MEN AND SUICIDE

My personal story and the stories of those left behind, with a deep dive into the construction industry

VINCE HAFELI, D.B.A.

Copyright © 2023 Vince Hafeli, D.B.A.

All rights reserved.

No part of this publication may be reproduced, copied, or transmitted in any form without the prior permission of the author.

This publication is designed to provide accurate and authoritative information and opinions in regard to the subject matter covered. It is sold with the understanding that through this publication the author is not engaged in rendering legal or other professional services. If legal or other professional advice or assistance is required, the services of a competent professional should be sought.

Dedication

I am blessed to have completed this life-altering journey. A long list of individuals and organizations stood beside me and encouraged me every step of the way.

The first thank-you goes to my best friend and wife, Stacey. She spent countless days and evenings alone while I traveled to research, gave talks in the United States and abroad, and carried out my mission. She has been nothing but supportive.

The following thank-yous go to my son, Brandon, and my daughter, Breeanna. Sharing my story that came forward in this process was challenging and therapeutic for the three of us. I apologize for not knowing I had put them through years of grief and struggles by not discussing my problems and asking for help.

To them, I apologize.

Two professors at the University of South Florida (USF) impacted me personally in a way that is difficult to describe. Dr. Grandon Gill spent countless hours with me over breakfast, providing guidance and direction. He is much more than a typical academic professor. He is a professor passionate about making the world outside university walls a better place.

Then there was Dr. Jennifer (Jenni) Wolgemuth. As soon as I type her name, tears come to my eyes. She introduced me to qualitative research and storytelling in November of 2021. We discussed my research in December, and she asked me to seek mental health counseling while conducting the study. Dr. Wolgemuth told me of a colleague who had conducted similar research and experienced emotional highs and lows, creating personal struggles. Engaging the services of a mental health counselor could prove to be beneficial.

Jenni has been with me every step of the way. I feel like I have a professor and a new friend for life.

My final dedication goes to those who shared their stories of loss with me. These are perhaps the most courageous and resilient individuals I have ever met. Their stories' power will help others navigate and find a path forward. The true intent of their shared stories is to educate organizational leaders on why they need to address mental health and suicide in the workplace.

Acknowledgments

I acknowledge my family at Ajax Paving Industries of Florida who covered for me while I was conducting my research.

This began with our Chief Executive Officer, Mike Horan, and the others on my Executive Team: Andy DeCraene, Scott Pittman, Ryan Fulmer, Mickey Cox, Dan Maitland, Matt Horan, Joe Minich, Matt Desotel, Clay Cross, John Savage, Mandy Kustra, Sandy Philipps, Craig Powers, and Christy Alvero.

I also acknowledge Jammie Simmons and Ginger Johnson who supported me during my research.

I could write an entire book on the quality professors I interacted with while conducting this research at USF, who impacted this project and my life. They include Dr. Joann Quinn, Dr. Paul Spector, Dr. Mathew Mularkey, Dr. Rob Hammond, Dr. Timothy Heath, Dr. Anol Bhattacherjee, and Dr. Al Hevner.

I acknowledge my dissertation committee:

- Dr. Grandon Gill
- Dr. Jennifer Wolgemuth
- Dr. Loran Jarrett
- Dr. Dirk Libaers
- Dr. Doug Hughes

I acknowledge members of my cohort who were part of my dissertation group:

- Paige Bridges
- Jason Maniecki
- Mathew Grace
- Haley Dunford

I acknowledge the following contractors who agreed to share their names.

Absolute Caulk	Nick Williams
Ace-Saginaw/Levy	Scott Seamon
Apollo Mechanical	Mike Ellis
Haskel Company	Jay Lemon
Hensel Phelps	Kabre Lehrman-Schmis
Jordan Foster	Tricia Kagerer
Lakeside Industries	Mike Lee
Mid-City Electric	Paul Lawson
Milestone Contractors	CJ Potts
Mosites	Jason Malatak
Murphy	Ricky Reams
Pacific Northwest General Contractor	Anonymous
RK Construction	Jon Kinning
Shamrock Electric	Kevin O'Sheaq
Vulcan Materials	Dean Sunas

Additionally, I thank the organizations interviewed that chose to remain anonymous.

Abstract

Mental Health and Suicide:

My personal story and the stories of those left behind, with a deep dive into the construction industry

By

Vince Hafeli, D.B.A.

This book is based on my journey and struggles with mental health and suicide, 12 qualitative interviews of those impacted by suicide (some of whom work in the construction industry), and numerous interviews and conversations with industry executives about how they address the topics of mental health and suicide in their organizations.

I wrote this book to share stories that illustrate the life-altering effects of suicide on those left behind.

I share my personal story and journey through life so that you, the reader, can understand that even someone with a perceived great life can struggle on the inside without exhibiting warning signs. If a suicide attempt can happen to me, it can likely happen to most anyone.

The literature review shows conclusively that suicide within my industry, construction, is high compared to other industry sectors and the rest of society (Centers for Disease Control and Prevention [CDC], 2020), with documented common suicide and suicidal ideation. A subset of the common themes tied to the industry includes stigma associated with discussing mental health and suicide, as well as prescription medication and self-medicating for injuries, and seasonal employment, which lead to a loss of income and depression.

The difficulty in overcoming some of these obstacles, and especially the stigma attached to them, is that this industry comprises a high percentage of males who have been led to believe they need to be mentally strong and not openly discuss topics such as mental health, including suicide. The lack of openness and reluctance to seek assistance have created an industry with a suicide rate of more than 4.3 times the national suicide rate, according to CDC statistics (Foundation, 2015). Two to three construction workers die daily of work-related injuries, while 10 to 15 die daily by suicide (CDC, 2020).

Qualitative interviews of industry executives highlighted a lack of knowledge and understanding about mental health and suicide in the horizontal construction industry (road builders, underground utility contractors, asphalt and concrete manufacturers, etc.). Overall, general contractors in the vertical construction industry (builders of homes, office building towers, high-rise structures, etc.) tend to be more knowledgeable about suicide and mental health.

Interviews with industry executives failed to document a theme of best practices in addressing mental health and suicide.

However, two common themes did arise:

Over 50% of the respondents indicated that they began addressing mental health and suicide after losing an employee to suicide.

100% of the respondents addressing mental health and suicide agreed that executive leadership must believe in the mission and openly discuss it with their employees on an ongoing basis versus a one-and-done basis.

Table of Contents

Foreword	1
Introduction	3
My Journey	5
Shared Stories	25
Mary's Story	26
John's Story	29
Terri's Story	32
Christine's Story	36
Danielle's Story	38
Dennis's Story	41
Stacey's Story	43
Eric's Story	45
Jennifer's Story	47
Bob's Story	49
Jamie's Story	50
Matt's Story	54
Summary of Those Impacted	57
Quotes and Stories Submitted to the Author	61
Industry Perspective	65
Industry Executive Interviews	71
Interview Themes	79

What the Numbers Say	81
Summary	85
References	87
Appendices	91
Appendix A: Executive Interviews Summary	91
Table 1: Executive Interviews	92
Table 2: Purposely Targeted Executive Interviews	94
Appendix B: Resources for Employers, Unions, and Multi-Employer Plans	96
About the Author	97

Foreword

Mental health and suicide in the construction industry takes us on a journey through the eyes of industry leaders—those who have experienced an attempted suicide or actual suicide, including me and the shared stories of—and impact on—those friends, family members, employers, coworkers, and others left behind, some of whom were associated with the construction industry.

I gathered the following stories and experiences as part of my dissertation for the Doctor of Business Administration degree at the University of South Florida, Tampa.

Twenty-five industry executives were interviewed to gain insight into their understanding of mental health and suicide awareness in the construction industry.

Twelve individuals impacted by suicide shared stories of their loss and the events that have forever changed their lives.

I have written this easy-to-read, nontraditional research book to encourage its use as an informative work of literature on how common the issue is, how it impacts almost everyone, and to understand where construction industry executives stand concerning this topic.

I intend for this book to inform industry executives and society that discussing this topic with their employees, friends, and family is how the stigma associated with mental health and suicide can be reduced.

The stories in the following pages are real, with individuals sharing their experiences—sometimes requesting to do so anonymously. The names have been changed while gender identity is shared to better understand the stories. The shared stories intend to raise awareness and knowledge so readers will be less judgmental of people struggling with mental health.

I share my journey as a suicide survivor and the impact of mental illness and suicide on my life and the industry.

Mental Health and Suicide

"Who I Am."

I am a serious man,
Who likes to get things done.
However, I am also a man,
That likes to have fun.

I am a dreamer that dreams,
Of how incredible this world could be,
If we could all have respect,
For each human being.

I am a loner who often sits,
In the darkness of night,
And ponders his life.

I often question,
"What will it be like,
When there is no longer life?"

I ask myself,
As I sit there in peace,
"Is this what it would be like,
If it ended tonight?

Will the pain of the world,
And my internal struggles,
And the fears and the fights,
Go away, that last night?"

I remind myself,
Before it all ends,
That I am a man on a mission,
A man on a mission to help all his friends.

That's who I am.

Vince Hafeli
October 15, 2022

"Who I Am" was inspired by Dr. Rob Hammond, University of South Florida.

Introduction

It took years for me to open up about the internal struggles and demons I held inside. By sharing my journey, the stories of those left behind, and presenting stories of industry leaders addressing mental health and suicide, I look to educate readers about individual struggles and how to make a difference. I have titled this book *Mental Health and Suicide: My personal story and the stories of those left behind, with a deep dive into the construction industry*. I hope to attract and educate readers about people's struggles, particularly those working in construction.

The shared stories are not unique to construction. Other segments of society, such as our youth, military veterans, first responders, dentists, and physicians, also experience a high rate of suicide. Although some of the stories in this book are not directly tied to the construction industry, I share them to provide a greater understanding of the impact on those left behind.

As you read, you'll be taken on a journey through my struggles with depression and suicidal ideation. You'll also hear the stories of 12 individuals who lost family members or coworkers to suicide.

You will hear stories of purposely targeted companies and how they are addressing mental health and suicide in the construction industry.

I ask you to read the book, share the stories learned, and take a moment to sincerely ask someone how they are doing. Take a moment to spend time with your children, grandchildren, or friends and see where they are and how you can make a difference.

Let the journey begin.

My Journey

I often contemplate how I reached the point where I was ready to take my life. My life has been full of success, but like most people, I have experienced failures and misery throughout the journey.

I begin by sharing my story to illustrate that I am a person you would not visualize as suicidal. As an observer of my life from the outside, I imagine many would seek to emulate me. My life has been filled with abundant success. However, if the observer could perceive my many struggles, I may be someone they would not want to be.

> Men in the construction industry die by suicide at twice the rate of civilian working men (16–64 years old): (Centers for Disease Control and Prevention [CDC], 2020).

Throughout my life, I masked many periods of sadness and darkness that I still struggle through.

> Studies show a positive correlation between chronic stress depression and suicide (Cassano & Fava, 2002).

My childhood was memorable and enjoyable. In my early years, we had ski boats and camping trailers and spent most summers at the Crab Orchard Yacht and Boat Club. Sounds fancy, but it was just a tiny marina on Crab Orchard Lake in Southern Illinois with a few spots for tents and camping trailers. I was so young that I do not recall most of those times.

The author at 7 months

My father while camping at Crab Orchard Lake

When I was five, I recall my father injured his back and was hospitalized and on morphine for quite some time. The doctor told my father he would require back surgery and could never ride in a boat again. This is when I first recall changes occurring in my life.

The surgery my father would require would no longer allow him to care for the beautiful two-story home where my mother, father, brother, and I lived in Du Quoin, Illinois.

I soon learned that we would be moving into a mobile home at Cherry Lake on the outskirts of Du Quoin. We would also be selling our boat and camping trailer. I do not recall what that meant to me then. Ultimately, I do not remember that the move negatively impacted my life.

Many joyous days were spent swimming in Cherry Lake and playing in the strip pits from the coal mining operations.

My father would soon begin to heal from his surgery, and before I knew it, he was well. So, what did my parents do? They built a barn and acquired five horses. I was now a seven-year-old boy living the life of a cowboy.

My father and me with one of our ponies in 1967

I recall opening Christmas presents in what must have been 1968: new spurs, chaps, a vest, and a saddle. The funny thing about that saddle is I could never use it. When Dad put it on my pony, it bucked like a rodeo horse. He never did learn to like being saddled. I always rode that pony bareback; sometimes, I even rode by hanging onto his mane with no reins. I recall times when I would hold on for dear life and scream in fear as the pony would race the larger horses back to the barn after a long ride. On occasion, I would hit the barn first with a massive smile on my face.

When I remember those days at Cherry Lake, I recall a day when my brother terrorized me. A small pond on our property extended beyond the property line. A barbed wire fence ran along the property line through the pond.

I was riding with my brother on his horse when he asked me to climb off and stand on the fence while he tightened the saddle. Once I was off and standing on the fence, he rode away and left me there for the afternoon. When my dad arrived home from work, I was on that fence, screaming and crying for someone to save me. Knowing my dad, I can only imagine how hard he was laughing inside as he took me off that fence.

The horses lasted for a couple of years and were then sold. My parents were never ones to go for very long without some recreational hobby.

It was not long before a new boat was purchased, and we were back in the boating business. Well, I say new; it was a small used cabin cruiser with an old Evinrude engine. Not much of a boat, but I learned to water ski behind it as we enjoyed camping at Pirates Cove Camp Ground on Crab Orchard Lake.

I do not recall having the boat very long because we swiftly transitioned into dirt bikes. My first one was a yellow Honda 50cc. Now I was no longer a Cowboy. I was living the life of Evel Knievel, an American stunt performer and entertainer.

Evel was one of my childhood heroes. I remember sitting in the back of an old Chevy truck at a drive-in movie theater, watching Evel jump his famous Harley Davidson over cars, buses, and whatever else he could imagine, such as the fountains at Caesars Palace in Las Vegas.

Another memory from that period is an afternoon on the Honda. I was racing on a track my brother and friends had built in the strip pits. I went off a ramp like Evel and hit a tree while airborne. So, what did I do? I did what any nine-year-old boy would do. I pushed the cycle home and hid it in the barn just before we sat down to dinner.

As I sat at the dinner table, I was terrified. Once we finished, I asked my mother if she would come into the bathroom so we could talk. I told her the story, and you can probably guess her reaction; she told me I needed to go and tell my father.

I quivered as I made the short journey from the bathroom to the dinner table, unaware of Dad's reaction. He responded, "It is your cycle, and if that is how you choose to take care of it, I am not sure what to say."

There was no yelling, butt whipping, or any repercussions. That was my dad.

A few days later, the cycle was repaired, and I returned to riding.

Three of my motorcycles – Did I mention that I was spoiled?

The next big move in my life was from Du Quoin to Johnston City, Illinois. I was about a quarter of the way through fourth grade when we made the move. Going from what I knew and my friends to a new environment was challenging; however, I quickly adjusted and made new friends.

Life, as I had known it, would soon begin to change. My father had a heart attack and was hospitalized for an extended period. My mother's brother, Uncle Burl, died while my dad was hospitalized. I remember someone saying that bad things happen in threes, and I know there was a third, but I cannot remember what happened.

My father's heart attack transformed my life. He had been a strong man—captain of the high school football team with a scholarship to the University of Illinois. He drove boats, rode motorcycles and horses, and worked on a drill rig prospecting for coal.

He was an underground coal miner at the time of his heart attack and spent his free time working on car engines and performing auto bodywork.

In many ways, my dad was my hero. I hesitate to use the word hero because, in my mind, that word elevates someone to a god-like status and only sets them up for failure. Let's say that I was very proud of my father and all he could do.

After his heart attack, all that he could do would quickly come to an end. He was now a man who would no longer be able to work. He was on many medications.

One night, I recall lying in bed crying as he and my mother fought. We, as a family, were struggling financially. Dad was no longer the provider. He said he no longer wanted to live. I sat and listened in horror as he flushed all his medications down the toilet. I was terrified. I thought I would soon be without a father.

> Studies suggest that a large loss in prosperity is more predictive of suicidal behavior than chronic behavior (Rancans et al., 2001).

I often wonder if that night was when I learned about people not wanting to live or move forward through their struggles.

Not only was his physical pain great, but his mental pain and anguish were equally or even more significant. He was sad, depressed, and irritable.

> Depressive disorders are characterized by the presence of suicide empathy, or irritable moods, accompanied by somatic and cognitive changes that significantly affect the individual's capacity to function (Shah et al., 2021).

I was now in sixth grade and forced to become the man of the house. I mowed grass, helped with laundry, and cleaned around the house. Dad's health did improve somewhat, but he never worked again.

But guess what? A few years later, we were back into boating—this time with a ski boat and a houseboat. Six great years were spent on those boats with family and friends from 1976 to 1982.

1980 - Houseboat at Crab Orchard Lake

I probably should tell you about my high school and college years. I was one of the few that enjoyed high school. I was on the football, basketball, baseball, and track teams.

I was fortunate to have dated "the pretty girl" during high school and into my second year of college. She was a cheerleader, played on the basketball and golf teams, and ran track. We had many fun years together, but ultimately, my immaturity ended the relationship while we were attending Southern Illinois University in Carbondale (SIU-C).

When our relationship ended, I went on a wild streak. I moved out of the house for the first time into SIU-C dorms. I spent many nights drinking Mickey Big Mouths, smoking cigars, and … those stories will be for another time.

During the spring semester of 1982 at SIU-C, I visited Daytona Beach with a friend (Steve) during spring break.

Spring 1982 – Schneider Hall at SIU-C

After a week of spring break, when it was time to return to class, I told Steve to go without me as I had met a girl from Michigan who was on spring break. I decided to stay and hang out with her before returning to class.

Once back at school, I informed my parents that I would move to Daytona Beach after the spring semester. I asked that they pick me up at the end of the semester and deliver me there.

That is what they did. My dad pulled up in front of the dorms in his 1970s-something green Buick station wagon, towing my 1953 Chevrolet truck with my 850cc Norton Commando motorcycle in the back.

1953 Chevrolet Truck

My Journey

The next phase of life was about to begin.

When I moved to Daytona Beach, I lived with my brother Rodney (Rod). Rod had resided in Daytona Beach for several years and quickly introduced me to the nightlife.

Perhaps I should mention that I hated my brother for the first 19 years of my life. Mom always said that hate is such a nasty and dirty word that it should not be used, so let's say we fought like cats and dogs, and on many occasions, I was less than happy to be around him.

I was nine years younger and probably more of a pest to him than he was mean to me, but it felt like he was constantly picking on and annoying me. I most likely got what I deserved, so let's say that I did not hate him; he just frustrated me.

1982 – Me bartending at the Beachcomber Club in Daytona Beach and cutting a birthday cake

In late 1982, my parents also moved to Florida. We were once again a family. There were fun times as I bartended at night, attended college during the day, and hung out on the beach in my spare time. The years from 1982 through 1984 were the wild ones. I am fortunate that I did not end up dead or in prison.

By 1985, I had settled down and was married for the first time. This is also the year I began working in the construction industry. I was so proud of my first job. I worked two hours daily at a pay rate of $4.50 per hour, breaking concrete test cylinders. That was the start of my professional career.

1988 brought the birth of my son Brandon, the joy of my life. We had a phenomenal relationship that lasted for years. More on that as we move forward.

My son Brandon - 1993

Things began to unravel in my life. In May of 1989, my brother was pronounced terminally ill. He would eventually pass on July 31, 1993, just past his 40th birthday. His passing happened to be on his youngest daughter's birthday, as she turned five.

My brother Rod

Fortunately, my dad did not have to witness his son's passing as my father passed in July of 1989, just weeks after learning my brother was terminal.

Before my father died, my wife and I would tell him he would again be a grandfather. He never saw that day.

I will once again say that, fortunately, he did not live to see the birth of what turned out to be twin boys because one passed within hours of birth, and the second was taken off life support after three days.

From May to December, I learned that my brother was terminally ill, my father passed away, and I lost two sons. Life was forever changed.

My struggles were not unique to me. Many individuals have had life experiences that were far tougher than mine. The difference is that I grew up as a product of the 60s and 70s, when men were told to be tough, strong, macho, and not share their feelings.

My skill in pretending to be emotionally strong was further amplified through being an employee of the construction industry, as it is a tough industry where men are expected to be strong and not bring their struggles, issues, and weaknesses into the workplace.

I recall standing outside at my father's funeral, telling friends and family that my father was better off now that he was gone. He was no longer living in pain and suffering. I told them he had lived a full life; he was 59. How much older should a person live?

However, that is not how I truly felt. Inside, I was devastated. Meanwhile, my professional career was beginning to flourish. Therefore, I did what men of my generation and men in the construction industry are expected to do. I was tough, strong, and macho and did not discuss my struggles with anyone – No One!

The one shining light in that period was the birth of my daughter in 1991. She was a sassy little girl. My memories of that time go back to me getting her ready for daycare each morning. She would sit on the living room floor as I put her hair into a little bow while she sat sucking her finger, watching Barney the purple dinosaur as we sang together. "I love you, you love me, we're …"

My daughter Breeanna

People told me there was a reason why all this death and sadness had occurred in my life. They said that God had a plan. I responded that if this was all part of God's plan, who would want him as their God? For me, life had lost all meaning. Death was not a significant event; it was just something that happened. From that point forward, I struggled to find compassion or feel sorrow for someone when they experienced a loss. I would say that people come onto this earth and then die. That is all there is to it. Suck it up and move on.

The struggles and tragic events in life can weigh heavy on the soul if not shared and discussed with someone. For 32 years, I never expressed my anger and hurt; it ate at me.

When I turned 60, someone asked me about my most challenging birthday. I thought and responded: I have not yet had one. They were puzzled by this reply. I explained that my life has become more relaxed and secure as I have aged, including being more financially secure. I can do more things with less stress now that I am 60 because of my financial situation. Thus, the paradox of life: young, healthy, and broke versus old wealthy, and broken down.

This security and relaxation have made my life less stressful and more enjoyable.

I then said the last piece of the equation is that I have no fear of death like many do as they age. In fact, I am pretty comfortable with dying as I expect peace and no more pain, and that will be a lovely day. Accepting that I am aging and not fearing the end, and in some ways looking forward to the end, leaves me at peace daily.

This is not a healthy state of mind. Perhaps I should talk to someone.

So back to the '90s. After my brother's death, I asked myself, what else can happen? I should not have asked that question because my mother was diagnosed with cancer and would die a few years later.

That was it. My immediate family was gone. At the age of 27, I lost my father and twin sons. My brother was gone when I was 31, and my mother was gone by the time I was 33.

Life had lost meaning. I did not realize it at the time, but I became a selfish individual. When my mother was near the end, she spent time in our house with hospice. I would take my son to the ball fields most evenings and leave my wife to care for my mother. That was selfish. I was not a good person at that time, and for that, I apologize.

Umpiring at Cooperstown, NY

I struggled to find happiness. From 1996 to 2002, I changed jobs six times. That was not me.

During this period, I did complete my bachelor's degree after 16 years, as well as my master's degree, so all was not lost.

I would be remiss if I did not mention the beautiful days from 1985 to 2002 spent with my in-laws. The holiday parties and days spent at Lake Como meant much to my sanity. However, as I reflect, I was an imposter covering my sadness and putting up a front.

In 2002, I had a new job opportunity, uprooted my family, and moved to Venice, Florida. I was now working for a contractor for the first time in my career. While life was good, it slowly began to unravel. I was not a great or perhaps even a good husband during this period. I was selfish and cared more about myself than I should have. The fights and struggles began to occur at home. I take responsibility for those bad days.

The arguments started to take their toll, and I began to wear down emotionally. My wife and I began discussing divorce. Life was terrible. Life was no fun. I was quickly becoming more of a failure in my personal life, at least in my mind.

> The risk of suicide has been associated with trauma and negative life events such as divorce (Kuo et al., 2012).

They say that when you discuss suicide, you should not go into the whys or the means because others may listen to the details of your why, tie it to their life, and justify an attempt at taking their own life, or perhaps it may trigger an emotion.

I will tell you that in 2007 — I do not even recall what time of the year, and it could have even been 2006 — I decided to take my life. I was driving in my truck to where I would end it. While driving, I talked to my wife on the telephone, and she said, "We know where you're going and what you'll do, and your son is on his way." I laughed it off and told her I would be home in a few minutes. I could not let my son find me a dead man.

I went home, crawled into bed, woke up the next day, and went to work as if nothing had happened; yet, the day was different. That morning when I sat at my desk, I pulled out four letters I had written to four of my most valued employees, thanking them for making me a success. These were my goodbye letters. More on those letters later.

I did not share my emotions and struggles out of fear and embarrassment. In fact, I had told our organizational leader I wanted to run the company when he was ready to step down.

How could I now tell him that I was struggling and made an attempt at taking my life? How could he trust me to lead an organization with several hundred employees when I could not manage my life? So I covered it up and kept it hidden.

> Vulnerable persons may seek to maintain their status as employed workers in part by avoiding contact with mental health professionals, however much stress they experience or perceive (Law et al., 2014).

I recall being bullied at work by a group of employees just before my attempt at taking my life. They would take emails that I sent in confidence and show them at their weekly meetings and laugh and ridicule me.

These emails were sent out of passion and love for my organization, and the fact that they would openly laugh and ridicule me was emotionally difficult. It weighed on me. It made me feel even more like a failure, leading to my emotional struggles.

In 2008, my marriage of 23 years came to an end. I felt both sorrow and relief. And as they say, life moves on.

My depression began to fade, and a new journey unfolded before my eyes. However, like most journeys, there would be some rough waves.

My relationship with my best friend, my son, was not what it had been. The divorce created distance between us. We have never talked about it, but I know he was angry, so I allowed it and let him go through his sense of healing and dealing with the event. This was tough on me. Would I handle it again the same way? Yes. I knew our relationship would heal, and it did.

I will speed up somewhat as most negative events are behind me. Or are they?

I married a wonderful woman who had become my best friend. We rode bicycles together in the rain and jogged together in the sun. We took trips on the Harley Davidson to the Georgia mountains and boat rides in the Gulf of Mexico.

My wife Stacey-2013

Yet with all this happiness, I carried the secret of my suicide attempt until 2021. The only people who knew were my ex-wife and son, or so I thought. I learned in August of 2022 that my daughter also knew, but we had never discussed the subject.

From 2009 to 2021, I accomplished many things. I completed 11 Ironman events, five Half-Ironman events, and a handful of Sprint Triathlons. I also purchased a few boats, one motorcycle, and a few sports cars.

Ironman Triathlon

Life should have been good, and it was, but I still carried the story of my suicide attempt within my being. That would soon change.

I began a Doctorate of Business Administration degree at the University of South Florida, where a professor challenged me in June of 2021 to find a more meaningful and complex dissertation topic than I had proposed. That challenge changed my life as I decided to research suicide in the construction industry.

Just before meeting with the professor in May 2021, I had again sunk into depression. I had trouble sleeping. I slept as little as two to three hours a night. I would tell people that work was terrible and life was not fun anymore. I contemplated selling everything I owned and moving away where life could be less complicated. I was ready to run away and hide. I was sad and hurting inside.

> Poor sleep quality is associated with a more than 60% greater likelihood of developing suicidal ideation (McCarthy et al., 2021).

After talking with the professor and deciding to research suicide in the construction industry, I felt empowered.

I felt I had an opportunity to research, educate, and share my struggles and those of many working in the construction industry. Through my many industry contacts and associations, I now had an opportunity to raise awareness and transform an industry. I quickly became labeled by ABC News as "A Man on a Mission."

> I decided to tell them about my suicide attempt.

On July 16, 2021, I told my Executive Team we would discuss suicide and mental health awareness on January 3, 2022, at our annual company safety day. I also did something else that day. For whatever reason, I decided to tell my team about my suicide attempt. I even discussed the letters in my desk drawer. I looked them in the eye as I told my story and told two of them that there were letters in the drawer for them.

It felt good to tell the story. However, there was little reaction in the room. There was no communication or conversation. The only sound in the room was my voice. You could have dropped a feather and heard it hit the floor. I did not expect anyone to say anything, but the awkward silence was strange.

Suddenly, 19 people knew. My second wife of 13 years, however, still did not know until one evening in October 2021. Stacey and I were sitting outside, and she looked at me, and I had tears in my eyes. She asked what was wrong. I told her, "I will tell you something you do not know." I told the story of my suicide attempt. I told her I discussed this with my executive team in July at our weekly meeting. When I was done, she asked, "How do you feel?" and I replied, "I feel like I can finally breathe. I feel like a load of bricks has been lifted off my shoulders."

As I began discussing my story and diving further into the research, I felt empowered with a passion I had never felt. For the first time in my life, I felt that I had a mission and a cause that I could use to help others avoid grief and misery.

One last event occurred that allowed me to share my story more openly. I was at a peer group meeting with several contractors when the topic of suicide surfaced. One of the contractors had lost two employees to suicide the previous year and wanted to discuss the events. An individual leaned over to me and said, "These people who die by suicide all have chemical imbalances or are a bit off."

> I figured that would be the last day of my employment with Ajax.

I immediately said, "Time out. Stop the meeting. I will tell a story not even the owner of my company sitting in this room knows." I figured that would be the last day of my employment with Ajax.

When we left the meeting, my boss put his arm around my shoulder and told me he was proud of me, and that was powerful. Guess what? I did not lose my job.

So why do I share all of these stories with you? There are lessons to be learned in my journey through life.

While I had what seemed to be a good childhood, difficult family events were happening, such as:

- Moving
- Stressful events with my brother
- Poor health of my father and eventual death at a young age
- Loss of twin sons
- Loss of brother and mother at an early age
- Bullying in the workplace
- Divorce
- When I relocated in 2002, my wife and I lost our social support system and did not adjust well to our new environment.
- In 2005, I began to experience psychological issues, such as low self-esteem. I also started verbalizing that I could never do anything right at home. To this day, I struggle with that issue.

> I share these stories to tell you that even people who appear happy can be struggling.

I share these self-reflections and lessons I have learned so that you can watch for the signs in others. I share these stories to tell you that even people who appear happy and well-off can struggle on the inside.

For many years, my life was like a house of cards waiting to crumble around me. I was not going to admit failure. I was not going to reveal my weaknesses.

How could I share my weaknesses? In 2003, I told the president of our organization that I wanted to lead the organization when he was ready to step down. How could I now share that I could not manage my personal life and expect that he would allow me to lead an organization of hundreds?

I would learn that this was completely untrue. When I finally shared my struggles, that same man said he was proud of me, and it took courage to share my story.

Where do I go now that I can finally acknowledge, discuss, and share my story? That is the exciting part: I am on a mission to *change an industry*. You will be surprised by how simple it is based on my research and recent lived experiences.

Shared Stories

When I decided to write this book, I knew I wanted to share the stories of those impacted by suicide—the ones left behind. I purposefully targeted individuals to interview who could share the loss of someone employed in the construction industry, such as Mary's father, and those in the construction industry who lost someone not employed in the industry.

Several stories relate loss for other reasons, such as John and Mary's son, who suffered from repeat head impacts (RHI) or head injuries. Dennis's story looks at the loss of two bothers.

In my journey, I was always embarrassed and ashamed. In the talks I give, I make sure people know I got to that dark night in 2007 through a journey over the years. It was not a single event that led me there.

The following stories show that we are all human. By sharing the stories of those in and those not in construction, I am looking for you to walk away knowing that death by suicide is nondiscriminatory and happens to all types of individuals, such as those in the following stories.

Mary's Story

"My Mother Adored My Father."

I was introduced to Mary while performing my doctoral research. Mary is middle-aged and believed that by sharing the story about the loss of her father, a lifelong construction worker, she could help others.

I sat in silence, looked across the table, and listened as Mary cried, laughed, and expressed anger and other emotions as she told me about her father, Tom. In the end, we both cried together.

My father was very good-looking, charming, and incredibly smart. His journey and success were remarkable if you consider his upbringing. He only had a seventh-grade education and grew up in a home with seven kids, an alcoholic father, and a mother with schizophrenia.

Alcoholism and schizophrenia eventually led my dad and his siblings to be taken from the home when he was about sixteen. The younger kids went into the orphanage; however, Dad was too old and subsequently lied about his age and went into the Marine Corps when he was sixteen.

Upon leaving the Corps, he eventually landed in the construction industry, building a career and starting a family. Mother adored my dad because he had a limited education yet was so successful and intelligent. Mom saw him as a giant, virile, good-looking man.

I now recognize that Dad had mental health issues but was so smart he hid them. There were also mental health issues with two of his siblings. One brother was an alcoholic and died of cirrhosis; another was a functioning addict, and a third led a life similar to my father's before passing.

I listened as Mary told the story of her mother receiving a telephone call two years before her father's death from her previous hairdresser, Janet whom she had not seen in 10 years. Janet said that Tom was at her house, had had a stroke, and had been taken to the hospital.

My family immediately went to the hospital, and Dad was there. We learned that Dad had been seeing Janet for months and had a stroke while at her home.

Mary described with tears being at the hospital with her mother falling apart while her dad discussed how much he loved Janet.

Once out of the hospital, Dad went into rehabilitation, where Mom cared for him. Three or four months passed, and Dad had another stroke at Janet's home. Dad did not fully recover from this stroke and lost his physical strength and stature.

In the construction industry, physical stature played a role and had played a role in my dad's success. He lost a lot of strength after his stroke, which was tough on him and led to mental struggles.

Time moved forward, and I received a telephone call from my husband, Brett. Brett told me that my father was gone. Dad walked out into the front yard and shot himself. Even with all that had been happening, it was still a surprise.

> Males die by suicide 3.9 times more often than females (AFSP, 2023).

When I reflect, I think my father had been asking for help, and we missed the signs. The one thing that I do know is that his death tore my family apart.

I recall that about a week before he died, he was struggling with losing his virility and the loss that comes with a stroke. While trying to help him through this, I recall my mother becoming angry with him. Could you blame her? I told Dad that God tried to give him a message, and he did not listen, so he hit him on the head with a shovel the second time.

Mom cared for Dad, but in some ways, she was not caring for him. Mom, at this point, was a bit like Nurse Ratched from One Flew Over the Cuckoo's Nest *(Mary said with sarcasm). After all these losses, Dad had an angry wife who turned to me. Dad started saying things that did not make sense, like some discussions about his safety deposit box.*

Dad said it was important that I got the safety deposit box, and he did not want Mom to see anything in it. He wanted me to be there first when something happened to him. I said to Dad, "Dad, you're not thinking of doing anything, are you?" He replied, "No, no, I'm not."

I told Dad he needed help with all this and should consider antidepressants. He said antidepressants are for the weak and have side effects.

Those are the things that I think about. (Crying) I wish I had done more than ask, "You are not thinking about killing yourself, are you?" I don't know. It's tough. What if I had done more than say okay when he brushed off my concerns?

One of my kids was a freshman in high school, and the other was a freshman in college, at the time of his death. All total, Dad had four grandkids.

My youngest does not say anything; however, my daughter, Jamie, is furious about what her grandfather did. Jamie is more enraged than everyone else. She sees what it did to her grandmother and me.

I am unaware of the impact on the other grandchildren, my niece, and my nephew. I mean, it had to have had an impact, right?

I want others to understand that this event impacted my relationship with my husband. I became very guarded and was not going to let anybody else hurt me. The emotion from the suicide taught me to keep things at an arm's distance.

Things are just different now in my marriage. My husband has always been a drinker; however, after the suicide, the drinking increased. I recall my daughter saying to her father, "If you are trying to do what granddaddy did, just do it with a gun. It would be a lot faster."

I did have a minister at my church that was helpful; however, beyond that, I received no counseling. I wish I had received some counseling; however, there was the cost and the uncertainty of what good it would have done.

My emotions go all over the place. There are times when it is just awful. I get mad at what he missed in my kids' lives. He should have been at all of the kids' graduations. He would have been proud of his grandson, who joined the Coast Guard.

I get so mad at what he missed. I get so angry at how it left Mom.

> I am not mad at my dad. I know that he had a lot of pain …

I am not mad at my dad. I know that he had a lot of pain that the family was unaware of and that he could mask it for only so long. His brilliance hid his struggles, which were eventually part of the final unraveling. I believe he had all of these facades built up: the good dad, the great employee, the manager, and you talk about how great he was on the job, and there is pressure.

The interview was over, and I turned off the recorder. Mary and I looked at one another. The last 17 minutes had been emotional. It became apparent that time does not heal all wounds. As time progresses and the grandkids grow, their grandfather is still missing, the wounds reopen, and the pain resurfaces.

We both stood up. As I walked Mary back to her office, she told me another story. When they opened her father's safe deposit box, they found his wallet. She said, "*You know you have to present your identification to the bank to get into your lockbox.*" With tears, she said, "*He left it in the box, knowing he would not be returning to the bank.*"

As we continued to walk, as Mary laughed, she told me a story about how her father loved the music of the Eagles and how she once danced to their music with her father's urn.

Mom remains crazy about Dad. She talks about him and still worships him.

We turned a corner in the hallway, and she told me a story about her mother selling the house.

Mom said she wanted to hang some new pictures of Dad when decorating the new home. I chuckled and said, "Mom, there will be no new pictures." Mom laughed. That laughter was the first I had heard from my mother in years.

Perhaps time does not heal all wounds. Somehow, though, the wounds become less painful.

John's Story

"You never get over the death; you learn to live with it."

I was honored to be introduced to Dr. John Gaal, a construction industry advocate on addiction, suicide, and mental health. This interview with Dr. Gaal opened the door to establishing a new friendship and advocate in my work to make a difference in saving the next life.

We began the conversation, and I was quickly educated on repeat head impacts (RHI) or head injuries an individual can sustain while playing youth sports.

John Jr. was quite an athlete in high school, where he was permitted to play soccer and football in the same season. As a former college soccer player, I was ecstatic that he and his little brother, Jake, would be allowed to play together.

John Jr. was a running back on offense and a safety on defense in football and spent most of the game on the field. In soccer, he played center midfield, where he was exposed to numerous head balls each game.

In his junior and senior years, he suffered four concussions, and in his senior year, he was knocked unconscious in a football game. When he came to, he was so discombobulated that he walked into the wrong huddle.

Two weeks later, he goes up for a head ball in a soccer game and is once again knocked unconscious. This is what the medical profession refers to as second impact syndrome (SIS). Often the results of SIS are not good. In his case, it proved to be true.

He silently struggled for the next six years, with our family unaware of the impact until December 2016, when he shared with us that he had barely graduated from college. I pushed back on that because I saw his transcripts, and he graduated with honors.

He told us he had a lot of help from his roommates in ensuring he was crossing his T's and dotting his I's in getting up and to class on time. He said it was like he was back in kindergarten.

He said that when he got to the classroom, he opened his book, which looked like a bowl of spaghetti, and he could not make heads or tails of the words on the page. He became a good faker and was able to get through college. He did not share these details until December 2016, when things began to spiral out of control.

Before he took his life on March 24, 2017, I knew what Chronic Traumatic Encephalopathy (CTE) was and how it affected people. His little sister was in a bad car accident in 2012 while John Jr. was away at college. He called home and told his mom not to cut costs and to ensure she got the best care possible because the concussions he had experienced in high school were taking a toll on his life.

My goal has been to generate awareness about CTE so others will not have to go through the pain, grief, and tragedy that my family has gone through. You never get over the death; you learn to live with it.

It seems Mary, my wife and John's mother, has recently begun to turn the corner. She now volunteers her time to organizations that help the people that John Jr. was interested in helping, which aids in her healing.

> For me, the tears were daily for the first three or so years, and were tears of sadness.

For me, the tears were daily for the first three or so years and were tears of sadness. For the past two years, the tears of joy outweigh the tears of sadness, and I have come to grips with certain things, such as self-blame. People must recognize they cannot do this alone; they must seek professional help!

His death took a toll on our family, with each of his siblings processing what had happened differently. Dana, his older sister, is the most analytical of our four children. She remains quiet to this day, while Jake, John's younger brother and best friend, took it very hard. John's passing left a huge hole. In my opinion, it took over five years for Jake to turn the corner and begin to talk and share stories about his brother. Leah, our youngest daughter and the baby, was away at college when John passed. She recently shared with us how she and John had discussed plans to travel the world, and now that has been taken away. We spend time with her and try to keep her in a good space. She is doing much better today than she has been for years.

Please make no mistake; it remains tough because several of John's friends are getting married, and a few are starting to have families. We are blessed he had so many close friends and often get invited to their weddings as John's proxy. I feel honored to carry on for John because he was close to them.

At his funeral, nearly one thousand people showed up; that spoke volumes about his character. When I was on the altar giving the eulogy, I knew it would be tough; however, it was not as one might think. When I looked into the crowd, I saw young and old, black and white, men and women all across the board, having both smiles and tears…indicating to me a life well-lived!

I have witnessed Dr. Gaal in person at events nationwide when he discusses opioid addiction, mental health, and suicide awareness. Dr. Gaal emotionally shares the loss of his son John, Jr. to better the world.

This is a segment from a piece prepared by Dr. Gall for the Construction Financial Management Association.

So, what does this have to do with the construction industry? Well, having retired at the end of January 2019, after about 40 years in the industry, and having served a vast majority of those years in the national apprenticeship and training arena, I can attest that Joint Apprenticeship and Training Committees across the U.S. and Canada have invested millions of dollars over the past two decades on recruiting efforts. Many of these marketing and advertising campaigns have targeted two populations: former military personnel and ex-college/high school athletes (mainly football players). A common (negative) thread between these two groups is the fact that many of these individuals who served on the field of battle and/or on the field of play were exposed to repetitive head injuries. To this end, those of us construction professionals tasked with keeping our workers safe now must think and plan beyond the physical aspects of safety. Make no mistake; we can no longer claim plausible deniability regarding this matter. In fact, we would be remiss in our duties if we do not also consider the mental aspects of safety henceforward.

Dr. Gaal, thank you for sharing your story and educating me and others on repeated head impact injuries and how it ties into the construction industry.

Terri's Story

"This too shall pass."

I was introduced to Terri by a mutual friend. Terri is the owner of an excavation and underground utility company.

On July 22, 2011, Terri lost her son Tyler at 25 to suicide.

Terri began the interview by saying, *"Please share Tyler's name in your book as it is relevant."*

At some point, when you talk to survivors or other family members or friends, many will tell you that, at a gut level, they might have known it was going to happen. That is hard for people to understand. It is like, no, no, we would have never thought that, but when you dig down, in our case, our family unit had been concerned about our son for many years.

> Transitioning from middle to high school is a critical time for many young men.

I would tell you that transitioning from middle to high school is a critical time for many young men. He was a sports guy. He hung out with all the, you know, jocks. He was on the wrestling team and lacrosse team. They all hung out, and drinking became a big deal in those circles.

Tyler was an introvert, and his drinking became his recipe for success. He could drink and become the life of the party. That is a very addictive place to be when you are a quiet kid.

Tyler had the highest SAT score in high school and never opened a book. He just knew the stuff. In his AP classes, he received a 4.0 or higher. I did not push him; he just did it to keep everybody happy.

His motivation was to keep his grades up so he could go out on weekends and party with his friends. We were not aware of how serious the problem was for quite some time.

When Tyler was a high school freshman, he approached me and told me he struggled with being shy. A friend gave Tyler a book to read. I think it was called being an introvert in an extroverted world. When Tyler finished that book, I remember he came to me and said, "Mom, this is going to change my life. This is awesome."

At the same time, he was dealing with the allure of alcohol and social gratification. He loved going out with his friends and being the guy. He was the jokester, the smart one, and he became very gregarious when he would drink. We did not fully comprehend how extreme it had become during high school as he managed to hold it together. At that point, I believe he was a functioning alcoholic. He began suffering from bouts of depression.

I was probably closest to Tyler as far as listening to his concerns and where he was because I am the mom. Right? We were very connected. There was a soul connection that was hard to explain. He knew he could tell me anything but did not always tell me everything.

I want to point out that when he was a freshman in high school, he was extremely gifted at anything tech, such as programming, hardware, and software. He was extremely good at coding and became immersed in video gaming. It became part of his addictive behavior.

That was in the early days when they started to network internationally, and it became a very quasi-socialized environment. Video games became a big part of Tyler's life. I believe when young people's brains are developing, some reprogramming occurs.

Tyler easily graduates high school and attends a most difficult engineering school, The Colorado School of Mines. Within a year, he flunked out.

The higher the stress level, the more his addictive behavior emerged. He is now on his own, and things begin to spiral down for him.

He would go through periods where he was up, down, and back up. He landed a summer job in the oil field on the construction side and made a lot of money. He also worked with his brother and me in our construction company.

Tyler is now 20 years old and involved in a devastating car accident that he should not have survived. Fortunately, he was alone. This was a wake-up call. For about eighteen months, he was in a program for DUI where he had random alcohol and drug tests. He lost his license and had no vehicle. Those eighteen months were probably the greatest gift.

He came out of that program, and I believe, one night, he just had a massive breakdown and took his own life.

Tyler did leave a note. When people leave notes that have taken their life, you will see sentences or words around pain. In his note, he said he could not take the pain anymore. It just was not worth it, and he needed to move on. His leaving was his version of freedom.

It was a very reflective note. Tyler did not blame the world; he was just in a lot of pain.

I get into these details because people need to look for warning signs, such as disconnecting from friends. We did not know all of this at the time; we learned after that he was isolating. He was becoming more alone and isolated.

The depression was setting in, and all the other pieces and parts were steamrolling. He did try to get help about three months before he passed. He reached out through the health insurance and his medical provider and received three therapists' names. Come to find out, all three of them either were not taking new patients, or he would have to wait months for an appointment.

We knew he was in trouble, and I think many people have individuals or employees around them who know something's wrong. Figuring out where the line is is the tricky part. How far do we take it? Do we intervene?

We had to go through a journey as a family. You usually find in families with a child that has passed or a young person, the divorce rates are pretty high. You have to come together as a family and not blame one another. You have to dig down and discover the actual lessons, figure out how life goes on, and find hope, forgiveness, and joy. It is a journey, and some people make it quicker than others.

It is troubling for the survivors if they hang on to the hate, anger, and grief for an extended period.

Tyler was the most amazing young man. He was bright, intelligent, and happy. He made a choice, and his choice was to leave. There was too much pain. We have since gone back and looked at his writings and just pieces of him that he left behind, and he was in a bad place that we did not fully comprehend.

I do not recall the events of that first year after his death, and I have a great memory. My world stopped. I could not breathe. I was stuck in the moment.

My husband and I became two islands. We were like two planets orbiting each other. We each had to grieve in our own way. We would talk, but we could barely talk about Tyler. Over the course, especially the first couple of years, we had to figure out how to navigate each other.

Some signs helped us heal. My husband went to close Tyler's bank account. Tyler had a tattoo on his upper arm that said, "This too shall pass." So my husband goes to close Tyler's bank account, and sitting on a desk at the bank is a card that says, "This too shall pass."

When my husband saw that card, it told him Tyler was okay.

Terri's story shares many valuable lessons.

One is that she and her husband survived the loss by "learning to navigate" one another. They learned to survive. They learned how to give one another space.

While Terri and I did not discuss this, my takeaway is that when one experiences the loss of a loved one through suicide, there needs to be time for individual grief and suffering before you can learn to grieve with even your closest loved one.

Christine's Story

"Wish I could have held his hand and told him I loved him."

Christine's father, John, was born in 1955 and worked in the construction industry his entire professional career. John was a product of the baby boomer generation, which believed the man of the house was to be the provider and should be emotionally tough and not discuss or share their struggles and emotions.

> Men in the construction industry will not seek mental health assistance. That has to change.

Christine begins to tell me her story.

I believe that men in that industry will not seek mental health assistance. That has to change.

He was the type of man who would give you the shirt off his back and ask, "What else can I give you? What else do you need?"

He volunteered two days a week at a nursing care facility and a thrift shop and loved helping others. When COVID hit, he missed his ability to give, and we believe this led him down the path of unrecoverable bipolar depression.

He was always an hour early for the party so he could help get things set. He was always there. He was the one that came to help get the yard ready for my son's fourth birthday party. I had another lady over helping that brought her husband. Her husband walked into the house, and he said, "Man, I don't know where you got that other guy to work here, but he works hard. I just saw him jump over your fence with one arm." That man jumping the fence was my dad at the age of sixty.

That was six years before he took his life. This illustrates you can be a physically strong man, but maybe you struggle mentally.

I believe that for people who take their life by suicide, there is not just one thing that happens; instead, it is a culmination of lifelong events. Some people have not been able to forgive themselves for mistakes or have not been able to talk to someone and work through it; that was my dad.

Dad lost five of his six siblings early. He lost a brother he was watching when he was young get hit by a car and a niece he was babysitting from SIDS. Neither of those two accidents was his fault.

My dad was bipolar and was not taking his meds. He told my stepmother that he wasn't a good man one day, and my stepmom asked, "Why would you say that? I wouldn't marry someone who wasn't a good man." He said, "No, I am just not." Ironically, he didn't realize he was such a good man.

He progressively felt more down. I wasn't aware. I knew he had had spaces in life where he felt that way. We had talked about it; however, at the time of his death, I was not aware.

I received a call from my stepmom. She said, "Christine, can you talk?" I knew something was wrong. She said, "Your dad killed himself, and Tommie found him."

I suppose the hard part about suicide is that sometimes people are remembered for that action and that moment when it is a combination of days of someone's life preparing for the event. There is a shame because there is a tendency for some to think that it was because the family perhaps didn't value that person or the family did not love them.

I can tell you that is not the case. I loved my dad, and I hope he knew. I did not get to say goodbye. I wish I could have held his hand and told him I loved him.

I was never angry with him. I am just sad that he suffered.

What was fascinating was how he prepared. There were little notes all over the house for my stepmom. That was fascinating because I couldn't believe he would have thought that all out.

It was painful for my stepmom because they had been married for forty years, and he was her best friend. She felt like he did it to her. I kept explaining to her and my stepbrother, who found him, that Dad would never have done that to you. If Dad were in his right mind, he would never have taken his life in his own home. Dad was very logical and intelligent.

After he died, I asked my stepmom if he was sick. He had looked ill for a while. She said she did not know; however, he had been losing a lot of weight and was very thin. I thought he probably didn't want to be a burden to anyone.

My twin sister, half-brother, and half-sister initially had a hard time while I did okay. I have been having a more challenging time lately.

I have the best closure because my dad and I were close and had a good relationship. I feel like I always tried to be there for him. We talked about things. I don't know if they can say the same and perhaps have more regrets, whereas I don't because I feel I did the best I could for him.

I know he suffered for a long time with his illness. I think that once men in construction retire, they lose value, and it hits them hard with a lack of purpose. I am grateful that he gave us the time he did. Sixty-seven is a long road to go if you're struggling in life. I think he waited, sadly, for all of his children to be as settled as they were going to be.

He was our hero, and we wish we could have saved him.

Like all interviews for this book, this one was recorded. I then transcribed the recording and carefully read through it. This story was relatable to me and my journey to that night in 2007. Christine mentions that she believes most people who decide to take their own lives do so out of the cumulation of life events. That was me.

1989, I lost my father and twin sons. In 1993, I lost my brother. In 1997, I lost my mother. In 2007, my marriage failed. As Christine experienced her struggles, nobody recognized these events or understood their impact.

I would like us to learn from Christine's story and mine. While individuals may not be exhibiting documented warning signs, the summation of events should be a warning sign in and of itself.

Danielle's Story

"I think the misconception that you only need to be on meds for a bit, or you don't need to be on meds at all, is something we can create more awareness around."

Danielle has become a friend in the recent past. Before my research, she listened to my struggles and journey and helped my construction organization with leadership training. It was only fitting that once I began writing this book, I asked her to share her mother's story.

Let me begin by asking that you use my and my mother's names in your book.

On May 8, 2020, when I was 37, my mother took her life while suffering from bipolar and dealing with depression. Throughout my childhood, she would have moments where she would be on a high and then a low. With bipolar disorder, you have these high highs and low lows.

She would have these highs where she would be excited and enthusiastic and other times when she would be depressed. I remember one time when I was in high school, and she took a sabbatical and sat on the couch for three months, just suffering from depression.

Early on, my mother and I had a very close relationship. I say this because my mom and I eventually had a bizarre relationship.

When I was two years old, my mom and dad divorced, and my mom kidnapped me. My dad went to pick me up, and everything in our house was completely gone. She had moved us like an hour away. My dad eventually found us. My mom made up some lies about my dad, and he ended up having supervised visits with me, which made it very difficult.

I didn't know my dad until I was fifteen. My relationship with my mother turned for the worse in my twenties. My mom, being bipolar, I never knew what I was walking into; she would be in an excellent mood, angry mood, or very depressed. She relied on me to elevate her mood, and our dynamic almost became like I was the parent and she was the child.

Ultimately, when I was twenty-three, she said you don't support me and don't love me, and you're not there for me. We jointly owned a home, and she kicked me out. That was the last time that we had a good relationship.

For the next thirteen years, we were estranged. The overarching message I would give people is that after much healing and counseling, I started to see my mom through a new lens. Instead of being so angry at and resenting her, I would see her as somebody who didn't have a very good childhood.

She came from a divorced family, and her mother went to a psychiatric ward for a year right after my mother was born. My mother's stepmom was not nice to her. I now look at my mom and say, "Okay, she was doing her best based on the hand dealt her. She was doing better than her upbringing."

I would say that when people in our lives are going through depression or people in our lives have anger and things along those lines, we try to take a step back and look at people from a different lens. Look at what might be *contributing to it. Instead of being judgmental of their past trauma, it's like what past trauma could contribute to it and what resources we can provide them.*

Another one would be to let the anger go. I put a guard up for a long time and would not get close to people. It affected how I showed up and my relationships with people. I had a tough time being vulnerable because I was protecting myself from more pain.

People in her life would say you need to go back to church, and you will be okay. I am solid in my faith, but what some people don't realize is there is a distinct chemical imbalance for some people who are bipolar. It is a chemical imbalance within their brain. Yes, your faith can help you get through things, but telling somebody to get off their meds and go to church is probably the worst thing they can do when it's chemical-related.

I know there were times when her friends would tell her to get off her meds, and then she would spiral and hibernate, and they wouldn't see her in those dark moments. They would see her in the good moments when she was on her meds.

I think that the misconception that you only need to be on meds for a little bit, or you don't need to be on meds at all, is something that we can create more awareness around.

That January, before her death, she attempted suicide and was in a coma for about a month. Then she went to a rehabilitation center to learn to walk and talk again and seemed to have recovered.

What people don't realize about bipolar and depression is that when people return to their meds, they are most vulnerable to suicide. They start low, and then they begin to feel better, and this better is what gives them the energy to follow through with suicide.

I think that's what happened. She got back on her meds, started feeling slightly better, and took her life.

I wonder if I had gone through counseling earlier in my life and if I had seen my mom through a different lens, would I have been able to help her?

We have experienced the loss. Now what do we do?

Do we live in anger? Do we live in fear? Do we question ourselves daily about what we could have done differently?

Danielle decided to seek counseling as part of her healing process. She made a powerful statement.

"The overreaching message I would give people is that after a lot of healing and counseling, I started to see my mom through a new lens."

My take is that counseling is the piece that aids in healing. I know it expedited my recovery when I talked to a therapist in 2022.

Dennis's Story

"My ability to cope came from the three-legged stool: faith, sobriety, and counseling."

Before beginning my research, I learned of Dennis's story through a mutual acquaintance. We talked a few times, and I was amazed at his strength after losing his brothers to suicide. What a tragic story.

I credit Dennis for taking his pain and grief and establishing the Half a Sorrow Foundation, which works to improve mental health for individuals and organizations by promoting honest conversations.

While I was away at college, my older brother Mark took his life in 1983. Mathew, my younger brother who was thirteen, was at ground zero. Mathew had just come home on the school bus. By a quirk of fate, our older sister Sheila, who did not live at home, stopped by that day. She got Mark out of the car that was in the driveway. Sheila was the oldest and got there first.

God bless her, but she had to deal with that. She tried to drag him out of the car. The car sat in the driveway forever. I told my dad to tow that damn thing and get it out of here.

I was at school eight hours away, went home for the funeral, and bolted right after. I could not get back fast enough.

Then the holidays come, and the first year sucks. The first Thanksgiving was only a couple of weeks later. I go home, and there is darkness over the house. Then it is Christmas, and darkness remains. It wasn't very good. Mathew was right there and was screwed up big time.

People in Mark's situation don't realize the ripple effect. At the time, the drinking age was eighteen. He was twenty years old and became reckless. So, guess what he did? He self-medicated.

If I could go back in time and say to Mark, "Listen, I know you are going through some stuff. But if you do what you are thinking of doing, Matthew will do the same thing eleven years later. I think that would have stopped him dead in his tracks."

Now I have lost two brothers to suicide eleven years apart.

What did I do? I drank a lot, and the drugs were there. I went on a binge and did not handle it well. It was like the Tale of Two Cities. When Mark died, I drank and did drugs, mad and depressed. Getting through Mark's death was like a bumpy dirt road for me.

When Mathew died, I decided to take a timeout from drinking. Sobriety was a big move as alcohol is a depressant, and I was already depressed—my sobriety and seeing a counselor made for a smoother ride.

Losing a child often creates difficulties that can destroy a marriage; however, my parents stayed married for sixty-one years. My mom would talk about them occasionally; however, my mother and father had trouble discussing Mark and Mathew.

In 2011, I came out and started speaking publicly about my brothers. I told my dad I was quitting my job and would speak full-time about my brothers. My dad looked at me and said, "You have a boy in college and another one on the way. Do you think it is a good time?"

After making this decision, I was asked to speak to soldiers at Fort Jackson about suicide prevention. Since my dad had been in the military, I called him to ask about his service career. My father asked me why I was asking these questions. I explained that I wanted to be prepared if they asked me questions. There was a long pause, and my dad said, "Go get them."

My sister Sheila put her emotions into a box and did not want to talk about her brothers. When I decided to do a Walk of Darkness for suicide prevention, Sheila was unhappy. She asked me, "What are you doing?" I replied. "I am walking and will also speak at the event." Sheila replied, "All right."

The walk was in New York, where our brothers were buried in the state park at Rock Lake. At the end of the walk, everyone went to a restaurant, had a little banquet, and celebrated Mark and Mathew. Sheila was reluctant; however, it was closure for us, and Sheila needed that more than anyone else.

My ability to cope came from the three-legged stool: faith, sobriety, and counseling.

Dennis is now a keynote speaker and educator who shares the loss of his brothers. We can all learn from his strength and resiliency. He has taken not one but two tragic losses to suicide and used them to fuel his desire to save the next person.

Dennis, I applaud you for your strength to stand on a stage and discuss your struggles in getting through the loss of your brothers as a means to help others.

Stacey's Story

"I would never wish the pain I have lived through on anyone else, nor would I trade it for anything."

Stacey is someone I met through an industry trade association that works for a highway contractor and wanted to share her story to help others. She was hesitant when I sent her the draft to review because of the pain it created when she saw her story in print. This illustrates how painful these losses are even after years of recovery.

Stacey, thank you for sharing.

I was fifteen when my father took his life on April 15, 2002. Looking back as an adult, I realize I grew up in chaos with a father who consumed alcohol to cope with his struggles. However, for the most part, I was very sheltered and felt safe, so it shocked the family when this happened.

My mom, Sue, and younger sister, Mary, took Dad's death much differently than me. I always felt that I had a deeper understanding of knowing that my dad's death was not about me. My mother and sister blamed other people, each other, and themselves. Dad's death was a struggle for Mom.

I had struggled as an immature fifteen-year-old who led a sheltered life. After Dad's death, I became an out-of-control teenager that was very depressed.

I felt shame about my father's death for a few years and was very self-conscious about being known as the girl whose dad took his own life.

As sad as his death was, his death saved my life when I became suicidal. I could not take my own life because of my experience with my dad. My life got dark; I dropped out of college, drank a lot, and was no longer a functioning adult. My 20s were unmanageable, and I could not hold a job.

As dark as things were, they became even darker when I received a DUI after driving down a road, losing control of my vehicle in Southern Georgia, and narrowly avoiding a tragic accident on a narrow bridge.

I was upset and mad at life and realized that God was not done with me and that I was here for a purpose. I continued on that dark path for a few more years before hitting bottom.

Hitting bottom led me to clean up my act. It motivated me on a journey of healing and change, where I gave up turning to alcohol and other unhealthy patterns and learned tools for success that I can apply to live in a way that brings joy and satisfaction.

My journey gave me compassion for the heartbreaking topic of suicide awareness, where I learned a lot and discovered ways to heal. I eventually found happiness working in the construction industry, where I found a forgiving culture regarding DUIs and being a college dropout.

My mother and sister never found an outlet or willingness to help themselves and continued to struggle. My salvation was exposure to an environment where expressing my feelings and emotions is okay.

My mother does not want to meet anyone or remarry, as she has not found peace inside like me, who learned that my dark path was my greatest treasure.

I always look at the world and think, "What can I learn today from this event?"

Stacey shares her story in a way that exemplifies why I wrote this book.

She discusses that she was suicidal; however, she could not take her own life because of her experience dealing with her father's loss.

Stacey did not know it when she made that statement, which is why I included these personal stories in the book.

Please listen to what she says. She could not take her own life because she knew the impact that the loss of her father had on her.

If you ever contemplate suicide, think about Stacey.

While I discuss throughout the book how the construction industry is tough and comprised of individuals perceived to be tough, this same industry is welcoming and forgiving.

Eric's Story

"His death opened a new door for me."

While attending an industry insurance meeting for my organization, an attendee heard of my story and research and asked if he could share a story with me.

He wanted to tell me about being 22 and the impact that he experienced when a close family friend took his life.

At the time, Albert was 33 with two children and going through a divorce. He was having a tough time with the divorce.

I can't even imagine what it was like with two little kids.

Albert worked as a gardener in the carpentry trade. That was his line of business for his entire career.

One day, on Christmas Eve, we were notified that Albert's dad had not talked to him in a couple of days. His dad went to check on him. When he arrived, he found him dead in the living room. He had killed himself and left letters on the counter for his kids, mom, dad, and ex-wife.

That was something that hit home for my entire family.

I come from a blue-collar construction family. That's what it is—blue-collar work. Everyone thinks that blue-collar workers have this tough facade, and they're tough, you know, these tough guys, but they're human beings, right? At the end of the day, we all deal with things differently.

I think that mental health hasn't been talked about or discussed nearly as much as it should have been for a long time. I believe that now sharing the information we have and the information we're getting will only benefit the industry and hopefully prevent suicides in the future.

I think death by suicide is an unbelievably selfish act. But you know, it always comes back to the question, what could I have done to prevent someone from doing it? Could I have talked to him? Could I have, you know, if someone was feeling suicidal, could I have dug deeper and asked specific questions to feel out their headspace?

I think the industry is doing a much better job. But we still have a long way to go with spreading information and doing things in the construction industry to prevent these going forward.

Suicide takes a toll on so many people, families, and friends. It has been nine years, and I still think about his death to this day, and I'm sure that his family thinks about it daily. Right?

My parents were very close to his parents, and they struggled. You know my dad is the kind of guy that doesn't show his feelings or emotions. I think I've seen him cry one time in my entire life. I don't think that's a good thing, either. Right?

He took it hard. My mom did as well. You know, my mom's a very emotional person. She took it very hard. It was easier for me to see the emotions she wears on her sleeve anyway.

His mother still posts on Facebook about her son. She just posted a picture this holiday saying she misses him and wishes he was still there.

His death opened a new door for me. When I know someone's struggling, whatever the case may be, I try to figure out a way to become more personable with them or compassionate and ask more profound questions that I might not have beforehand.

It cannot be emphasized enough how important it is to ask meaningful questions. It is easy to ask, "How are you doing," and receive a quick, "I am good," and move on with your day. True communication takes more than that.

It is also important to observe physical characteristics and signs. When I am struggling, I tend to gain weight. Food is my go-to place for comfort. When my mind is in a good place, I lose weight.

For some, it is alcohol or drugs. For others, it may be isolation.

If you are in doubt, have a private conversation with them. If you need guidance on how to begin the conversation, dial the national suicide helpline at 988. They will guide you on how to initiate the conversation.

When deciding whether or not to ask someone if they are struggling, have no regrets.

Jennifer's Story

"I get my drive from thinking about my brother and mom and practicing gratitude in bringing good to the world."

Jennifer is a brilliant young woman I met at an industry event. She listened as I discussed mental health and suicide in a health and safety meeting and stopped me afterward and asked how she could help.

I asked if she would be willing to share her story.

When I was four years old, my older brother, who was fourteen, died by suicide. I was the one who found him. It was a traumatic event as I was only four years old. I did not understand what had happened.

It had a traumatic impact on my family. It was mentally stressful for them to lose a child in that way. His death devastated both my father and mother.

When I think back to that event, it somehow instilled many of my values and defined who I am today. I value inclusion and want to support other people.

As a kid, I recall my mom speaking about him being bullied in school. That was one of the things that she attributed to his death. Those conversations ended on my tenth birthday when my mom passed.

So as a little kid, I interpreted it as people were so mean to him at school that he killed himself. That made me feel like, wow, I never want anyone to feel like that. I never want to be mean to anyone. I never want other people to be mean. I want to go around the world to hug everybody and make everybody feel better.

When I reflect on my childhood, I feel like I was drawn to people who were outcasts to help bring them in and make them feel less like outcasts. You know, kids like to tease each other a lot. I got teased a lot as a kid.

When my mom passed, I latched onto academics to cope. I had this sense from people at a young age that everyone expected me to fail after those traumas. I was this kid who had a lot of weird stuff happen. I did not have a traditional family, so that made me different.

I wanted to prove them wrong, do well in school, and prove myself. I also did not want people to judge my dad and think he had done a lousy job. I wanted to be a shining kid who did well so that it would reflect upon my dad.

I tried to positively influence my parents' lives by being one of those kids who consistently tried to make things better because they were sad. In school, I became passionate about things that I thought would enable me to have a positive impact. Ultimately in my career, I've stayed focused on trying to have a positive impact.

I get my drive thinking about my brother and mom and practicing gratitude in bringing good to the world.

As I reflect on Jennifer's story and her wanting to share, I realize that in my talks on this topic at industry events, it now has a ripple effect throughout many segments of our society. While her experience with death was not from construction, her willingness to share and educate came through a construction industry event.

Jennifer has taken her loss and struggles and is working to leave a better world behind. She is passionate about her work with the environment and the impact she can have on people.

The takeaway is that we all must find our way of coping. Mine has become public speaking and writing this book. Jennifer's is the environment.

Let's change the world and how we discuss mental health and suicide so that fewer will have to find ways of coping with suicide.

Bob's Story

"Unfortunately, it took losing our friend and colleague to make it happen."

Bob works in the aggregate and mining industry. While attending an industry event, I learned that Bob lost a coworker. I asked if he would share his story.

Bob was quick to say yes. He told me that we must do something to save these people in the mining and construction industry.

Tony, a good friend I had known for years, was a trusted business colleague and one of the nicest people you would ever meet that worked in the construction aggregate industry.

I never knew Tony had anything going on. He was a good family man, and I would always talk to him. Every conversation was about how the kids were doing or where they'd been on vacation. He just always led me to believe that he was happy and healthy.

He had to take some time away when we got into the pandemic. It was, you know, kind of a hush-hush; it was confidential. The boss called and said, "Hey, Tony is stepping away for a while, so he won't be accessible. Route all your calls to Sandy."

When he returned during the pandemic, I reached out to him and said, "Hey, listen, I don't know what's going on, but you have my full support if you ever want to talk."

He was very upfront and honest in saying he had a tough time. "When we all went into solitary confinement, and I was home alone or with my wife and kids, sometimes it was difficult."

Tony sought out help. The tragic thing about it is when he returned, we thought everything was okay. And he, again, spoke about it openly.

I got a call about four months later one evening, and Tony had left the office and taken his life. It was really tragic and still pretty raw. He was the person I had been closest to, and I knew his family and what he was made of.

Since then, we have made discussing mental health part of our safety meetings.

> Construction managers die by suicide at a rate of 45.7/100,000 (Peterson, 2020).

Construction is a tough industry, and we do not discuss mental health because of the stigma. It isn't easy to have those conversations when talking to guys working in a rock quarry or the construction business. Right?

Now there are posters up everywhere. I lead safety meetings with my folks to ensure they care for themselves and their families.

Unfortunately, it took losing our friend and colleague to make it happen.

I often talk to people at events who assume this is a blue-collar issue. It cannot affect white-collar educated individuals. Can it?

Suicide and suicidal ideation do not discriminate. Tony was different from me in many ways yet similar in others.

This story reemphasizes that we need to look, listen, ask questions, and not assume people are okay just because of their job or financial status.

Let us all decide today that we will not wait until we lose a colleague, family member, or friend to address mental health and suicide in the workplace or at home.

Jamie's Story

"We never shared the weak moments, and I regret not doing that to this day."

Jamie is a friend whom I have known for over 30 years. We both worked in the construction industry during this time. When I began this research, Jamie asked if I would be interested in interviewing him for the study and book, as he had lost his brother, a construction worker, to suicide in 2013. Since we were friends, imagine my shock when I realized I was unaware of his brother's death by suicide.

This further illustrates the profound silence around the topic of death by suicide.

Jamie begins to tell me his story.

People in our industry shared with me they had that issue. When I was the division manager, two people told me they were going to commit suicide. I had to use the Baker Act on one of them.

[The Florida Mental Health Act, commonly called the "Baker Act," allows for involuntary examination initiated by judges, law enforcement officials, physicians, mental health professionals, and close friends and relatives. Under the Baker Act, examinations can last up to 72 hours after a person is deemed medically stable.]

Then I lost my brother, who worked for a construction company laying asphalt. So, I have dealt with it both professionally and personally.

At thirteen, my father was shot and killed in front of my brother, mom, and me. My brother was ten at the time. The pain was gut-wrenching.

So, my brother and I came up ill, frustrated, and confused, but we had a bond that we were always there for each other.

We didn't talk about the pain. When I did and the tears would well up, I would stop talking because I didn't want men to see me cry. The fear of shame and showing emotion in front of men was something my brother and I held onto for years. Looking back, it was wrong that we kept everything inside.

We're these tough guys going through life and didn't talk about our dad, who was murdered before us. We were always angry at society and God for deciding we didn't need a daddy.

Fast forward. My brother, who has two children, had an excruciating divorce. The divorce was terrible for him, especially since he and I came from a broken family and always wanted to be there to raise our children. We wanted to raise our children and have our family and never break them up because of the pain we've been through.

I always thought that my brother was emotionally as strong as me. I guess I miscalculated because I lost him and didn't address things with him had I known.

> Those entering the "culture" of the disabled are overwhelmed initially, and they fail in their efforts to adapt; they think of death as a solution (Brodsky, 1977).

About three months before he took his life, he had been dealing with a medical injury to his arm and was looking at disability. He was having a tough time and started having this negativity more than ever. He would start crying and having soft moments we had never experienced together since my father's funeral.

I was going in my direction, and he was living his. Mine went exceptionally well financially, with family, kids, homes, and property, while my brother struggled. He was barely getting by after his family was taken away.

I felt for him but was committed to keeping my stuff straight. I kept giving him the rules, where you must do this and do that. I was very firm, always telling him to get his act together. I was good at dictating how things ought to go.

In the last three months, he had softened up. He went to church with me one day, and we sat in a church side by side for the first time since my father's funeral. I went home and told my wife that it got me.

We had never shared the weak moments, and I regret not doing that to this day. We always played tough with each other.

Mama was worried about him. He's an hourly worker on a paving crew, went through a divorce with two kids with child support, and the world is just eating his lunch.

I thought I had a good plan but hadn't figured out how badly he was hurting.

Then, at 7 a.m. on March 12th, 2013, my wife walked back into the house through the front door crying. I knew I had lost my brother before she got to me. My whole world reverts to the anger I feel for what happened to my father.

I was the one who had to tell my mother. I had not heard her scream that way since my father was killed.

I have a mother that has a murdered husband and a son that died by suicide. It is difficult, to say the least, and the pain she feels every day is unimaginable. I was worried about losing her.

After losing my brother, I started analyzing everything. I had lost him and was at a loss because how I didn't do what I should have done. I went to therapy and said, "I need to know what you think of all I've been through because I just lost my brother, and I'm confused."

I learned from her that I cannot live with the guilt of my brother.

I wish I had known the pain he was in. I just wanted him to be tough. I thought he was, and the next thing you know, he's lying in a coffin.

I regret assuming that my brother was as tough as he used to be. I regret that to this day. I could have saved him, maybe.

Some people are here today because somebody did speak to them. And something happened to change their mind just by what they saw or heard. I don't know if I could have done anything differently that would have kept him here.

I have taught myself not to live with guilt and let it emotionally hurt me or my family.

I should have gotten help when my father was killed. What I mean by help is I should have talked about it and not kept it inside because that was not healthy. I've learned that living with guilt is very difficult.

To this day, I wish I had done things differently where he's concerned so there would have been the opportunity for him to talk.

I've tried to help his sons. His oldest son does have up-and-down moments.

I continue to help my mother to this day as she will never recover from losing a child, much less by suicide. Now that I have children, I can't imagine the pain.

Jamie is one of the most caring human beings that I have met. He cares about people and is an advocate for them.

It was apparent during the interview that while being compassionate individuals, men in this industry can also be tough. Brotherly love can be tough. Jamie said, "I was very firm, always telling him to get his act together. I was good at dictating how things ought to go."

Jamie went on to say, "We never shared the weak moments. I regret that to this day. We always played tough with each other."

There is a valuable lesson for us here, particularly leaders in the construction industry. Let us learn that we can be better leaders by sharing our weak moments and learning from our weaknesses just as we learn through "SWOT Analysis"—strengths, weaknesses (both internal looking), opportunities, and threats (both external looking).

Matt's Story

"As Long as They are Talking, They are Breathing, So Keep Talking."

Matt works for an additive supplier that provides chemicals to the construction industry. I learned of Matt's loss through a friend. Matt asked to share the loss of his son to help others understand the pain and its longevity.

Matt began talking.

I'm Matthew Joseph. My son was Joseph Matthew. We called him Joe.

He was our only child.

He was exactly 20 years and one day when he took his life.

He was in college at the time. He started at RPI, Rensselaer Polytechnic, in Troy, New York, and after three semesters, transferred to Worcester Polytechnic.

Joe was a very, very smart individual. He was one of those kids you know at a very young age that he's above average regarding intelligence. He was speaking in sentences and paragraphs at the age of one year.

It was a bit of a clue when he started walking and talking the same week. People would look at him and ask, "Did that baby just talk?"

He had a perfect score on his SATs. He was just really bright. He was not socially awkward, although he was never exactly like his peers. He was into soccer when he was younger. We never had any real teenage problems with him. If there ever were two times in my life that he challenged me, it was at the ages of three and thirteen.

Nothing in our world leading up to his death gave us any clue about what he would do. It was a big shock because we thought things were okay for the most part.

We suspected he had broken up with his girlfriend.

I am away in Florida on business and got a phone call. He is gone, and I have a long flight home.

I am now dealing with the aftermath. You know it will be a long ride, but you don't know how long.

I called my best friend at the time, who lived down the street, to ensure my wife wasn't alone. He lost his wife a few years earlier. When I arrived, he told me I had a long road ahead. Those words stuck with me.

> Talking to people about his death helps me better understand my feelings.

After 12 years, you find some peace. One of the things that helps me understand my feelings is talking to people about his death.

It was tough on my marriage, especially with only one child. It is tough when you lose a child to any circumstance, but when you lose one to suicide, you somehow blame yourself. You wonder why you didn't see it or why they couldn't come to you.

After time goes by, you realize that I did what I could, and even if I could have done more, it wouldn't have even stopped it. Right? When somebody is determined, you can only postpone it.

I deal with it by telling people my story when they ask.

It lends to your message. If you can talk about it, it changes things and the dynamics.

As long as they're talking, I always tell people they're breathing. So, keep the conversation going. It's an uncomfortable conversation. It isn't easy, but what happens when you speak openly about it is remarkable.

A friend from high school I had lost touch with contacted me on Facebook when my son died. He told me he had three children, could not imagine going through something like that, and was sorry for my loss.

I left a simple reply and said that I hoped you never have to go through this.

A year later, I learned her son had taken his life. I went back to Facebook Messenger to reach out to her and saw my last message hoping she would never experience this type of loss. Okay, now, what do I say following that?

I apologize for the fact that she had to join this exclusive club that we belong to.

He was in school to be a mechanical engineer. It was not his passion; it was just something he was very well suited for.

Fortunately, for two summers in college, he worked for the company where I worked. I spent time with him at work, where he saw my world, which was fun. I'm very fortunate, and those are the memories that I have.

My wife and I survived the experience and will be married 31 years next month. She is now able to talk about his death. She doesn't talk about it quite as openly as I do.

In general, we were both living happy, fulfilled lives. It took a long time to get there, and there were years that I didn't think I'd hear her laugh again.

You know, it's one of those things; when it happens, you are just kind of like you're not prepared for the emotions of hearing the laugh.

It always helps to cry over good things now and then.

How do they do it? How do Matt and the others wake up each morning and go through the day? Matt says he is part of an exclusive club.

Matt, please realize that although you and the others who shared their stories may all be members of an exclusive club, you are an inspiration who helps others make it through the day.

I thank you and the others for your strength in sharing.

Summary of Those Impacted

The interviews have been completed, and the stories are written. I ask myself, what is the takeaway?

Those interviewed shed tears of laughter, sorrow, and pain. There were moments of joyous memories and periods of silence.

I was educated not to show emotions when conducting these qualitative interviews. I was instructed not to nod "yes" or "no" or acknowledge agreement or disagreement as this may influence the answers and direction of the conversation. Laughing or crying might alter the validity of the answers.

While I did my best to show no emotions during the interviews, it wasn't easy. Was my preparation and guidance in conducting these interviews appropriate for this topic? How can you sit and listen to these stories, be stone-faced, and not show emotions or a comforting smile? Wouldn't that be cruel?

I did not follow the guidelines during many of these interviews as I cried with the people sharing their stories. Their pain and suffering brought back memories and emotions of days in my life. As I listened, my mind sometimes drifted into thoughts of what would have been had I taken my life in 2007. What would have been the impact on my son? Daughter? Wife? Uncle? Nieces? Cousins? Coworkers?

Other times, I listened intently, held my emotions in, and strategically planned my next question. Then I exited the interview and found a location to shed my tears or perhaps sit in the darkness of night in my backyard, replay the day's events in my head, and cry silently.

I want to apologize to those during whose interviews I held my emotions in check. I meant no disrespect; I was trying to be a professional and do as trained. I had tears for each of you at some point, and I do again as I write this paragraph.

To the readers, you will never know some of these individuals by name as they asked to remain anonymous. I will share that they are all emotionally strong individuals with remarkable resilience. Some of them have established foundations to carry on the memory of those they have lost, while others still have difficult periods where they are just trying to make it through the day.

After I prepared a draft of the interview and asked those interviewed to review it for accuracy and to make sure they were comfortable with the story as written, one requested that I pull the interview from the book. They no longer felt comfortable sharing their story. They expressed that they are still learning how to cope with the event.

Let me emphasize some points from the interviews that you just read.

One of the mothers interviewed explained how she makes it through difficult times at work:

There are times when I am struggling. My coworkers and supervisor allow me to say that I am struggling, and they give me my time and space.

As I look to educate leaders of organizations on creating a caring culture, I urge them to listen and learn from what this mother had to say. More importantly, learn from her supervisor and the organization's underlying message. They have acknowledged and continue to allow and support this mother to grieve during the challenging periods.

During one of the interviews, I told a mother that people say suicide is a selfish act. She was quick to put me in my place.

My son was not selfish. My son was and had been in emotional pain for many years. He did not take his life out of being selfish; he just wanted the pain to end. So do not tell me that my son was selfish.

In my eyes, she is correct. Why did I ever say that to her?

When I think back to my struggles in 2007, I had this pain and aching inside that I just wanted to end. Nothing I tried was making the despair, pain and hopelessness disappear. I should be empathetic and understand how her son felt better than anyone. There were messages of pain and sorrow as the survivors described how they were impacted and the emotions they dealt with and still experience today.

> **If you or someone you know is struggling, do not be a coward as I was. It is okay to ask for help. Dial 988 or text 741741.**

I now go back to the "why" regarding the impact of the loss on those left behind. In my mind, I question if I successfully shared stories of those impacted by suicide, and if I did, will they make a difference?

These stories are real.

The reason behind my wanting to share these stories is the message. I seek to educate people on the impact of when someone decides to take their life. The effect lasts a lifetime. The pain and suffering never end.

Does it lessen? The answer is yes.

Does it ever become bearable and acceptable? For some, yes; for others, no.

"You never get over the death; you learn to live with it."

Quotes and Stories Submitted to the Author

The shared stories were emotional and impactful as I gathered the information for writing this book. In addition to the interviews, I gathered many more stories from people through emails, text messages, telephone calls, and in-person visits. I want to share some of the stories and comments collected between March 2022 and April 2023.

I showed my vulnerability in a webinar with the Women of Asphalt, not realizing the impact it would have on others and me.

I received the following email from a woman telling me she no longer had to live in shame. I challenge leaders from all industries who read this book to learn from this email and lead with vulnerability and empathy.

"I no longer have to live in shame."

I just wanted to thank you for sharing your story today during the Women of Asphalt webinar. Sometimes we say or do things that touch other people's lives or even save them without us knowing it! And that is a VERY big deal in today's world.

In my life, I have had quite a few family members that attempted or succeeded in suicide happening in their lives. I even saved my mother from it as a teen and cannot say that I never considered it during some very hard life experiences.

Your sharing your story makes me feel less ashamed of those feelings.

This email came from a woman sharing about her daughter and how she was cutting herself. What a powerful message I conveyed because I discussed my struggles and weaknesses.

"You wonder how you failed."

When my daughter was in high school, she started cutting herself and ended up in a psychiatric care center. As a mother, you wonder how you failed your child, and when you see them wearing a sweatshirt to cover their arms, you panic.

After listening to your talk today, I have to say that I hugged her tighter and longer when I saw her.

The talk reminded me how precious life is; you truly do not know what someone is going through.

I was invited to the Asphalt Pavement Association of Indiana Convention in December 2022 to share my story and discuss my research. When you stand in a room and present to a group of strong, tough construction workers, you sometimes wonder how the message is received.

Out of over 9,000 construction workers I have presented to, there was push back from just one. That is a positive for leaders to hear.

The workers in the industry are hungry for this information and want to share their struggles.

I was attending a meeting in Dallas, Texas, on January 2023, when the event organizer asked me to take ten minutes and discuss my mission and research. When I returned home, I received the following email.

"I should have paid more attention."

I apologize for not paying closer attention. I did not write down the name of the gentleman that stood up at the conference and spoke about suicide and mental health. I should have paid more attention.

It is amazing how I just heard about the statistics and received a text message 48 hours after returning home about someone struggling and deciding to take his own life.

People often do not listen because they are unaware that it is such big issue both in construction and nationally.

"Your ability to bare your soul and show the crowd that a real man can speak about having poor mental health drove the point home."

Thank you for delivering one of the most powerful speeches I have heard. Your ability to bare your soul and show the crowd that a real man can speak about poor mental health drove the point home to the hundreds of attendees and me. The topic of construction worker suicide and mental health was on everyone's lips throughout the conference.

"I'm gutted."

My close friend took her life today. I'm gutted and don't have words. I can't believe she is gone. Thank you for having the empathy and fortitude to sit with families and hear them.

What do you do with this message? First, you cry. Then you write back to the person, tell them how sorry you are, and offer a hand.

Then you think, why the hell am I doing this? Isn't enough, enough? How many more people am I going to encounter who are losing someone?

In one week, three contractor friends told me they had lost employees to suicide that week. I ask myself, "When will it end, and how much more can I take?"

"Lots of tears in the room."

That was the quietest I had seen the room in twenty years overseeing our conference. It is also the only standing ovation I have witnessed, with many tears in the room.

At the bar, I talked with a second-generation owner of a member company and his Quality Control Manager. The owner said he understood the importance of the presentation, but it made him a bit uncomfortable. He said he did not know anyone who had ever taken or tried to take their life.

The QC Manager told him he almost did after work while at the plant several years ago. He was struggling and sat in his truck with a pistol for a long time, considering what to do.

The owner was moved and discussed his need to continue to be okay.

That conversation would never have happened without the discussion and presentation about this topic.

When you are at the bottom and beginning to feel depressed, you receive a message that lifts you, and you see you are making a difference through these interviews, presentations, and discussions.

"It was very, very impressive and heart-touching."

Mr. Vince, I watched your TEDx video; it was very, very impressive and heart-touching. My significant other, whom I am with now, lost her baby and has been there.

I hope that everybody will watch this video and make a difference.

This is one of the best things Ajax is doing for our people and community in a work environment. I want to thank you from the bottom of my heart.

The link to the TEDx talk, "Discussing Mental Health and Suicide in Construction," is https://youtu.be/zrNdAT2vuaI.

As I sat and had another evening conversation with my wife about my contact with someone else who lost someone to suicide, she asked, "Does it ever end? I never knew that it hit so many as often as it does." I reminded her that someone in the United States takes their life every eleven minutes (AFSP 2023). *Every eleven minutes…*

Will it ever end? No, it will not.

Can we reduce the numbers? Yes, we can through authentic leadership and learning from the shared stories and messages that I received.

Industry Perspective

When I decided to research and learn about mental health and suicide in the construction industry, I began conversing and asking questions as I visited people throughout the industry. What I quickly learned was that most leaders are unaware of the statistics. They are unaware of the numbers. They are shocked and find it hard to believe that more workers die by suicide than by injury on job sites.

I recall breakfast with three executives at the National Asphalt Pavement Association (NAPA) Annual Convention. During our conversation, I learned that one had lost an employee to suicide the previous year, one lost his father to suicide, and yet another had lost two employees to suicide.

Once we were in the conversation, they were surprised it was an issue in the construction industry. They thought the suicides were unique to their organizations.

The stories are not unique. The stories are not unusual. These are the stories that I learned as I began to interview executives.

As I began the research, I maintained a journal documenting my journey as I headed down this qualitative research path to try and help others.

After leaving the NAPA convention, I headed to West Palm Beach for a meeting with seven contractors. At that meeting, I soon learned one of the organizations lost two employees to suicide the prior year. I also learned that two individuals in the room each lost a sister to suicide.

I said to myself, "It just never seems to end."

How do we make a change? What steps need to be taken?

Organizations need to overcome barriers such as a lack of leadership support. People must stop saying that discussions about employee mental health and suicide have no place in the workplace.

Some say there are no safety regulations requiring we address these matters, so why would we? They think, "They are union members, so the union should handle it. It's not affecting their performance, so why should we care?"

During my research and conversations, I learned that as you talk about mental health and suicide, people desire to learn, be educated, and act.

In my journal, I documented stories and messages. One such message read:

> *We had eight employees from our company at your presentation on suicide in the construction industry at the Asphalt Pavement Association of Indiana Winter Conference. The talk and education made a big impact on us. We're already discussing what we can do within our organization to start the discussion. Keep sharing the information. More contractors need to hear the message and get involved.*

While the research was on the construction industry, I soon discovered that this is an issue that runs deep within our society. I want to share a story from a teenager.

I served on a scholarship selection committee for high school-age women. The following are excerpts from the required letter a student submitted with her application. The letter addressed the scholarship's importance and what it would mean to her.

> *At 18, I struggle to find my identity and question who I am. I feel the constant weight of uncertainty, which often leaves me lost, confused, and overwhelmed. I fear that if I do not fulfill others' expectations of me, I will be seen as a disappointment to people. Navigating my discovery is my most challenging obstacle.*
>
> *The expectation placed on me by my family defines their ideal image of me and set forth an impossible reality of how my life should be. I feel pressured to know everything and be their perfect daughter.*
>
> *These expectations are setting me up for failure. They are a constant reminder that everything I am is not good enough. I know they mean well when trying to do what they think is best for me, but have they ever wondered why I want to do what I want to do with my life? What are my opinions? How do I feel?*

Industry Perspective

After trying to fit an impossible image, you cannot recognize yourself anymore. Behind my smile, I feel pain and guilt.

There are days when I feel alone, even when people surround me.

I grapple with the concept of self-worth and self-love.

> Teen suicide is up 150% since 2008.
>
> In 2021, 10% of 9th–12th graders reported at least one suicide attempt in the previous 12-months (AFSP, 2023).

I'm tired of wearing a mask and lying about my feelings. I'm tired of pretending my mind isn't stuck repeating self-degrading and hurtful thoughts. I'm tired of the constant triggers and panic attacks.

I look in the mirror and see tears and trauma, a broken person that cannot be fixed. I desperately long to feel whole and complete. I hope to become proud of who I am and comfortable with myself. Others' thoughts and opinions are overwhelming.

To find happiness, I will begin to fight for myself and the freedom to explore who I can be, for the right to celebrate who I might be, and for the time to figure it all out.

I share this story with you because I expect thousands, if not millions, of people to have similar stories. What will this young lady bring to the workplace? In addition to the knowledge and skills she will gain as she continues her education, what about her mental health and coping skills? As she enters corporate America and even family-owned businesses, she may find it overwhelming that mental health and suicide are not properly addressed or addressed at all.

As an example, I share a story from one of my experiences. I serve as a trustee on a national board for a foundation that provides money for those killed while working on a construction site. During a board meeting in February of 2023, a discussion occurred about how much money should be in the foundation account to remain solvent.

The question was, "Are we collecting excess funds, and could the funds be used elsewhere in the trust?" One trustee suggested that excess funds could be used to educate the membership on mental health and suicide. Another trustee in the room replied, "Those funds are for burying workers and not for educating them."

Wow! What a hurtful statement. While it was painful, it was accurate. Based on the by-laws, the funds could not be used for training and education as written; however, the by-laws could be modified.

As the days passed, I could not help but wonder, have some of these old gray-haired men lost touch with their employees? Have they lost touch with their trade associations' goals? Have they lost touch with society? Have they lost touch with the struggles of today's world?

Educating these types of leaders is the mission, and the obstacles we must overcome.

I sat at a roundtable discussion at a mental health summit in March 2023. I listened intently as participants discussed mental health and caring and debated what a nurturing environment looked like.

My response to the group was this:

ABC News has labeled me as a Man on a Mission. I am on a mission. I am on a mission to educate industry leaders on mental health and suicide in the workplace and how to elevate our game and care more for our employees.

What I do not want to be known for is the man that lobbied for handing out cotton candy and gumballs every day at work.

Construction and many other businesses are challenging, demanding industries where we must have some strong safety and operational rules.

We need to acknowledge that, at times, we must be firm. We may need to raise our voices (yell). That does not mean that we do not care.

What we need to eliminate is the bullying effect. We need to stop being judgmental when humans express their emotions.

In the end, it is just about being a good person.

Industry Perspective

There needs to be a change, and the organizations that make the change will have a competitive advantage.

Based on my qualitative interviews, conversations, and lived experiences, I know that leaders will learn that once they begin addressing mental health and suicide in their organizations, they will have a resilient, loyal workforce.

When we transitioned to addressing mental health and suicide at my organization, I received stories like the following:

> *I appreciate being employed here. I have to say that I have listened to your message about suicide, and I had some serious thoughts about it recently. I've gotten into a rough patch by doing anabolic steroids while pushing to become a bodybuilder. I have wonderful children, and I'm married to a beautiful woman. I have absolutely everything to lose at this stage of my life. I was processed out of the military last year due to health issues, which took a big toll on me mentally. I guess I'm saying I've been one of those individuals in the front row listening to your message, which means more than you probably ever know, brother. Thank you. Thank you so much for everything you do for us, and I look forward to hearing your message again.*

A fellow contractor sent me this story:

> *I watched your TEDx talk and shared it with my co-workers to discuss when and how we would show this. After watching, one in the room told me he had lost both his father and brother to suicide and his son spoke to him about how he had also thought of suicide. There were only four people in the room. Right then, we decided this was not about when and how but how quickly we could get this out. Thank you for sharing. I admire your courage and praise for what you're doing.*

Then there was the story of a young man participating in the American Foundation for Suicide Prevention Construction Hike for Hope, where I addressed the attendees about suicide in the construction industry:

> *Thank you for the information and talk on Saturday at the Hike for Hope. I was there. I've lost an uncle, two high school friends and struggled with suicide. It means so much what you and others are doing. Thank you.*

These are some of my lived experiences and industry stories that have been shared with me.

Industry Executive Interviews

As I began my qualitative interviews with industry executives, I selected contractors across the United States in horizontal and vertical construction. I quickly learned that most executives in this industry are unaware of the number of suicides in construction or that construction has the second-highest rate of suicide of all industries (Centers for Disease Control and Prevention [CDC], 2020). They are unaware of the issue and the struggles.

However, I heard some positive success stories in my sampling, for instance, from organizations like Balfour Beatty, with programs and initiatives to address their employees' mental health and concerns.

Balfour has programs that focus on providing resources to employees on identifying the warning signs of suicide and how to intervene and get assistance for someone struggling. They encourage employees to seek help if they are experiencing mental health issues. They have toolbox talks and safety meetings dedicated to suicide prevention, where they distribute these materials and resources.

The company also offers a wellness program focusing on overall health and wellness, including mental health. They support employees struggling with stress, anxiety, or other mental issues. The organization has created a culture of support and understanding around mental health and the workplace.

Other companies reported that they have a physical wellness program in place. Still, some shared that they do not have specific initiatives or programs to address mental health or suicide prevention for their employees, even though one employer indicated he lost an employee to suicide in 2012.

Some indicated that mental health is not a focus for their company and is not given the same attention as physical health.

Some companies reported not having lost an employee to suicide since inception, although several employees have personally experienced the suicide of someone they cared about. Yet, the companies have not implemented specific programs or training related to mental health and suicide awareness. They report, however, that they are beginning to research and learn more about the topic due to the recent awareness campaigns within the industry.

Then there are stories from organizations that once had a robust mental health and suicide awareness campaign and program led by a strong individual. Still, the program ended when that individual left the organization. Those remaining understand that they should probably restart it.

I interviewed some great leaders, such as C. J. Potts from Milestone Contractors.

C. J. has worked in the industry for 38 years. He discussed his weekly visits with his crews in the field, where he stands with these individuals, and asks how they are doing. He believes it is essential to communicate with and understand the employee's perspective to create a safe and healthy work environment.

Another selected organization discussed losing one of its attorneys to suicide. Their story illustrates that suicide can impact an organization and society regardless of the person's role or stature.

Most CDC data would lead you to believe that suicide in the construction industry is tied to blue-collar workers, yet based on this organization's story, it can strike all levels. This company began addressing mental health and suicide after the employee's death. They now have regular toolbox talks and frequently visit their field operations to discuss mental health and suicide.

Their story of losing an employee and beginning a mental health awareness campaign is not unique. More than 50% of the companies purposely targeted told similar stories. They started addressing mental health and suicide after losing an employee, not before.

Many success stories come from leaders showing their vulnerability. Kevin O'Shea with Shamrock Electric is a great example. Kevin shared an executive leadership presentation that he gave:

> *Write this down. Write down 988. Here is my cell number. Write that down, also. The first number will get you to the National Suicide Prevention hotline. They have professional counselors available 24/7.*
>
> *If you call my cell, I am not a professional counselor but a sympathetic ear to listen to you.*

Kevin now closes every email with the tagline, *"Your mental health and safety are as important as your physical health and safety."*

Other employees at Shamrock have also begun signing their emails with such taglines.

During Kevin's executive presentation, he shared with his employees that he has attention-deficit/hyperactivity disorder (ADHD). He told them that he is not defined by his ADHD.

Kevin was diagnosed in the second grade and took medication to control the symptoms.

ADHD makes my job difficult, but with the aid of medication, I'm able to make it through the day.

Kevin discussed suffering from depression and how he is not defined by it and let the group know that he believes in and uses therapy.

I purposely targeted Absolute Caulking and Waterproofing as an industry leader in addressing mental health and suicide. They shared the strategic mental health and wellness initiative they established in mid-2020. They reported that it requires time, money, and resources to ensure a Total Worker Health (TWH) environment, but being safe and more productive pays off. Absolute now looks at its systems each year and sets strategic goals to fulfill the company's needs regarding TWH. They have made decisions on their insurance lines with mental health in mind. The company also provides training and certification for its employees around mental health.

I asked Absolute the top three things a company should do to address these issues. They listed them as follows:

1. Establish a budget.

2. Communicate often and consistently with no shame or judgment.

3. Train and educate employees.

When I asked Absolute what comes to mind when I say mental health, they quickly said:

Compassion, empathy, meeting people where they are, and trying as hard as possible to support those needing assistance.

Another purposely targeted organization was Apollo Mechanical. Apollo is a privately held company with over 2,700 employees specializing in HVAC, piping, and plumbing that has been in business for 32 years. Apollo works in several markets, including nuclear, data centers, microchip markets, schools, residential services, and industrial food processing.

Apollo, like most companies, began addressing mental health awareness only recently. In 2020, the decision was made to focus on mental health and suicide prevention after the team realized that death by suicide is a significant problem in the industry. The company executives were on board with the decision, given their belief that a healthy worker is safer and more productive.

Apollo sent some staff to be QPR (Question, Persuade, Refer) certified and made a commitment for half of their weekly safety meetings to be health and suicide-related.

When I asked Apollo, "What comes to mind when I say mental health," they indicated it's "emotional stress," meaning people are struggling emotionally and mentally.

> ... leadership was on board with the decision to begin addressing mental health and suicide ...

It is important to note that Apollo's leadership was on board with the decision to address mental health and suicide. Still, as a privately held organization, they struggle with financial constraints. Those implementing the program realized they could not ask for more time and money beyond the safety systems they already had. The staff showed the leaders that they could organize their existing safety training and add mental health and suicide awareness into the overall worker safety program.

Apollo's message to contractors is that you must have a solid safety program before you begin the mental health program.

I asked Apollo what advice they would give someone wanting to start the mental health and suicide awareness journey:

You must first get leadership buy-in and ensure the executive team is on board, supportive, and willing to carry some messaging. Having a level of messaging from the executive team, middle management, and the ground floor is essential.

Beyond that, it's an assessment of where your organization is in terms of education. What do people know after they review the benefits that the organization has in place?

Ensure you have the resources to back up your conversations because people will come to you and need help after you begin having the conversation. Make sure you are prepared with the answers.

Yet another purposely targeted organization was Mid-City Electric, a commercial electrical and tech company with 550 employees, of which about 450 are union workers.

Mid-City says they began addressing mental health a year after losing a foreman to suicide. They initiated the program by rolling out toolbox talks and crew meetings. They then picked an employee assistance program (EAP) for the field program and began VitalCog Training with their employees. VitalCog is a program that teaches organizations to proactively address the early warning signs of suicide in the workplace.

I asked Mid-City why they began addressing mental health. Like so many other organizations, it was because they lost a foreman to death by suicide.

I also asked them what they would list as the most powerful things they've done to address mental health and suicide.

> Allow people to be authentic and vulnerable.

Allow people to be authentic and vulnerable. That has been a game-changer.

Our culture has gotten to the point where before our foremen write somebody up or give a warning, they reach out and say, "Hey, what's the best way? What can we do to support them? How can we support that guy because I think he's struggling?"

That happens all the time. That creates an environment where we want people to know it's okay, not to be okay. That's a big thing.

Create opportunities for vulnerability, especially in the field, to supply ongoing education and training that you regularly have.

One organization recognized nationally as a leader in addressing mental health and suicide is Hensel Phelps, a general commercial and federal healthcare contractor with approximately 3,500 employees; they have been in business since 1937.

I asked Cambrie, a project superintendent for Hensel Phelps, when they began addressing mental health and suicide prevention. Like many, they initiated such programs three years ago after losing an employee to suicide. During the interview, Cambrie highlighted that their Chief Executive Officer had posted a video on the importance of mental health and suicide awareness in the company. He was proud to say that the employees' reception to the training has been positive.

I ask Cambrie what three things Hensel is doing that others should also do. Cambrie quickly answered:

1. *Employee training on recognizing and approaching people.*

2. *We are a visible leader in the industry. We proactively participate in mental health summits, share our work, and learn from others.*

3. *The company supports us and our mission.*

Mosites, another purposely targeted organization, engages in commercial, institutional, and recreational renovation and heavy highway construction projects.

I asked why mental health was important to the organization. They mentioned several reasons:

They indicated that the employees initially held their emotions close to the vest, but they have become highly receptive and involved with continuous support. They report that they are in a good place right now; however, they said they cannot become complacent as people come in and out of the trade daily and must continue to educate.

Another purposely targeted organization leading the charge was the Murphy Company Mechanical Contractors and Engineers. Murphy has been in business for 115 years and has 1,000 employees. Approximately 700 are craft workers, which are 100% union.

I interviewed their Vice-President of Safety and Quality, Ricky, and asked if he views mental health as a positive or negative:

We look at mental health in a positive light.

We know that people struggle with it, and putting it in a negative light drives the negative perception and stigma.

People don't want to express themselves when struggling with mental illness, such as depression or anxiety, when they have a negative perception of it. So, we put it in a positive light and say that this is entirely normal that everyone has the same struggles.

This should not be anything to be embarrassed or ashamed of.

Murphy initiated their mental health and suicide campaign after losing an employee to suicide.

I purposely targeted RK Industries, located in Denver, Colorado. RK has been in business since 1963. They have approximately 1700 employees and are 100% nonunion.

During my interview with their Chief Operating Officer and Executive Vice President, Jon, I asked why they began addressing mental health and suicide awareness. Jon indicated they were a very early adopter and began addressing the topic before 2013.

We were unconsciously incompetent when it came to this. We've been affected by suicide in our organization, as most everybody has been affected by suicide.

Jon stated that VitalCog training is required for the HR and safety people, with some training being led by their president and general manager. Training for non-HR and safety employees is optional.

I asked Jon what he thinks when he hears "mental health."

Compassion.

I asked Jon what he thinks of when he hears the word suicide.

Avoidable suffering and silence. Long-term decision on short-term problem.

Interview Themes

The interviews and stories from the past 18 months establish a narrative. They tell a story of an industry underinformed regarding mental health and suicide. Yet they also tell the story of an industry that has recently begun to show positive movement.

My interviews and conversations revealed six prevalent themes:

1. In general, vertical contractors were early in adopting mental health and suicide awareness strategies. I expect this is partly because vertical contractors rely heavily on ironworkers, who have a suicide rate of 79.0 per 100,000 (Peterson, 2020), whereas horizontal contractors rely less on ironworkers. Trade organizations such as the Associated General Contractors and the Associated Building Contractors that represent vertical contractors were early adopters in addressing mental health and suicide, leading to this industry segment being a leader.

2. Regional differences exist in how these issues are or are not being addressed. In general terms, the leaders are in Missouri, Colorado, Washington, and Oregon. This statement paints a broad stroke as progressive and forward-thinking contractors in other states also address the topics.

3. Most organizations tend to begin addressing mental health and suicide after losing an employee to suicide.

4. Successful organizations have support from the top of the organization.

5. Organizations not developing mental health and suicide programs indicated they were unaware that mental health and suicide are issues within the construction industry.

6. The organizations with the most success are typically overseen by the safety department, with the support of their HR staff.

The construction industry is harsh. The employees are macho and have a strong front that has historically been expected of them.

My travels, interviews, and conversations indicate that once organizational leaders are willing to address the topic and say they will create a caring culture, the employees greatly appreciate it. Employees begin sharing their stories, discussing their struggles, and asking for help and guidance.

While not part of my research or my conclusions, I can't help but think that mental health will significantly tie into and improve our safety risk on projects. Workers being more mentally engaged cannot help but support the physical aspects of safety.

What the Numbers Say

The Centers for Disease Control and Prevention reports the following:

- Adults 35–64 account for 46.8% of all suicides, and suicide is the 8th leading cause of death for this age group.
- Men 75 and older have the highest suicide rate among the Centers for Disease Control and Prevention bracketed age groups.
- Young adults ages 10–24 account for 15% of all suicides annually, totaling 7,126.
  - Young adults have the highest rates of emergency department (ED) visits for self-harm. In 2020, ED visits for this age group were 354.4 per 100,0000, compared with 128.9 per 100,000 among middle-aged adults ages 35–64.
- In 2021, 9% of high school girls reported attempting suicide during the previous twelve months. Suicide attempts were more frequent among girls than boys (12.4% vs. 5.3%).
- In 2021, 6,146 veterans died by suicide. Suicide was the 13th leading cause of death among veterans and the second-leading cause among veterans under age 45. Veterans have an adjusted suicide rate 57.3% greater than the nonveteran U.S. adult population. Veterans account for about 13.9% of suicides among adults in the U.S.
- In 2021,
  - 48,300 people died by suicide in the U.S.
  - 12.3 million adults seriously thought about suicide.
  - 3.5 million adults made a plan.
  - 1.7 million adults attempted suicide.

- Suicide rates increased by 37% between 2000 and 2018 and decreased by 5% between 2018 and 2020. Rates nearly returned to their peak in 2021.

- Construction ranks as the second-highest industry group in deaths by suicide.

- Construction and extraction (mining, quarrying, and oil and gas extraction) rank the highest occupation group in deaths by suicide.

AFSP shows the highest suicide rate among middle-aged white men with men dying at a rate 3.88 times higher than women, with an average of 130 suicides daily. White males accounted for 69.68% of suicide deaths in 2020 with more than 50% of these by firearms.

If you are a numbers person, the above should be of concern.

If you are like me, a numbers person who uses data to help better the lives of others and your organization, what do the numbers mean for the construction industry? Why are the numbers so high?

Construction can be demanding, with employees relocating from job site to job site. These moves can create an environment of instability with employees families and coworkers. The work hours can be long and fluctuate from day to nights and nights to days. This fluctuation can lead to sleep deprivation and injuries. The oscillation is also disruptive to an employee's home life.

When employees are injured and unable to work, there is no pay. Change in financial status poses a risk for suicidal ideation (Turvey et al., 2002).

When injured, employees are often prescribed opioids and begin to self-medicate with alcohol or illegal drugs.

Mood disorders, alcoholism, and personality disorders are the three most important risk factors for completing suicide (Yaldizli et al., 2010).

Annual regional unemployment occurs within the industry. Construction workers in cold-weather states can be unemployed for up to five months a year.

The long periods of unemployment create a "short work season" where the workers can expect to work long shifts up to seven days per week. These long work periods occur when children are on summer school break, creating stress in home life by being absent.

The industry is physically demanding. Equipment operators are subject to repetitive movements and work in the extreme summer heat. The physical demands can lead to workplace injuries, but employees often work through their injuries because the industry embraces a tough-guy mentality. They seek medical attention, receive prescribed medication, and quickly return to work.

Often, however, workers do not report injuries and self-medicate with alcohol or illegal drugs or the abuse of prescribed medication such as opioids. Fortunately, in recent years, many types of mobile construction equipment have been equipped with air conditioning to help create a friendlier work environment. Due to worker compensation rules and regulations, attitudes towards medicine and returning to work have changed somewhat in recent years.

Nevertheless, the industry can be highly stressful. Most work is obtained in a low-bid system that generates lowprofit margins. Employers push employees to meet the schedule while performing quality work without injuries. This pressure begins at the organization's top and filters down to the lowest levels.

Employees in this industry have typically chosen not to discuss or ask for assistance due to the stigma associated with mental illness and the low use of employee assistance programs (Boss, 2020). While more companies have implemented employee assistance programs, many do not consider utilizing them due to the associated stigma.

Studies show construction workers might be at higher risk of suicide because of economic and interpersonal concerns (McIntosh et al., 2016). Distress experienced by workers at times of uncertainty, particularly those in less-skilled jobs (Meltzer et al., 2010), creates a loss of self-worth, leading to suicide ideation. In addition, the industry employs many military veterans who experience social isolation, poor social support, medical conditions, and feelings of hopelessness that contribute to suicide (Janssen, 2001).

While the industry can be challenging, it can also be rewarding. In Texas, Florida, and Georgia, four out of the five most prevalent construction occupations had higher median pay than the median for all employees in the state in 2019, and five out of five in California, New York, Kentucky, and Michigan had higher median pay (Simonson, 2020).

The industry creates a culture of teamwork and family. Employees do not typically work in isolation; instead, they are part of small units ranging from two to 15 on average, creating an attractive work environment for U.S. military veterans. The industry also creates an environment where high school-educated employees can succeed and generate a six-figure income. In a few short years, patient employees who ask questions and have a strong work ethic can advance into mid-level and upper-level management.

The heavy civil industry keeps the nation's infrastructure system at the ports, highways, and airports moving forward. General contractors create masterful high-rise projects, aviation buildings, and medical facilities, to name a few. Environmental contractors work to restore polluted waterways into pristine estuaries. Power line utility contractors bring electricity to our homes and businesses; plumbing contractors allow us to utilize fresh water and dispose of it through a sanitation system. The industry is a proud one that keeps America moving.

We leaders are now responsible for creating a caring culture to reverse the upward trend in the suicide rate and maintain a vibrant, physically and mentally healthy, strong workforce.

Summary

Where do we go from here? We all make choices in life. Do you lay this book down and go about your life as usual, or do you change your organization? Do you change your life? Do you change how you lead and communicate with your family?

If you are a parent, I hope the suicide statistics on our youth scare you. They should scare you. I have several friends who have either lost their children to suicide or have rushed them to a hospital to save them.

The pressures on our youth from social media, academia, and society have proven relentless. Kids can no longer be kids. Why do they need personal cell phones at a very young age? When did we decide that it was okay for a family to sit at the dinner table with everyone on a personal device playing games or texting with someone? What happened to dinner table conversations? Social media bullying takes place 24 hours per day, 7 days a week. How do we end that?

What about workplace bullying? Have you ever been subject to it? I have. I was bullied just before my suicide attempt. I did not realize I was at the time, but through therapy sessions and self-reflection, I realize I was. Did that push me to that night in 2007? I am sure it was a piece of the equation.

If you are a construction industry leader or executive, you have a responsibility to become educated on mental health and suicide and the resources that are available to your organization. I have provided a list of resources in the appendix.

Addressing mental health and suicide awareness in construction is easy and inexpensive. Here is a breakdown of what it might look like:

- Year 1
  - Support begins with the leaders of the organization. Leaders must be present, visit job sites, and have open conversations about the initiative. I recommend they first attend some training, such as CIASPs Living Works 90-minute online interactive tutorial on suicide prevention.
  - Commit to four toolbox talks. These can be downloaded at no charge from the CIASP website.
  - Purchase 988 hard hat stickers.
- Year 2
  - Continued leadership support.
  - Go to monthly toolbox talks.
  - Look at VitalCog or similar training for supervisory personnel.

We all now have an opportunity to make a difference. The question is, will you?

I have dedicated the remainder of my life to helping anyone who asks for it, along with guidance. The burden is now on you as to which path you take. Do you walk away, or do you leave with an impact?

Like ABC News said, "I am a man on a mission." If you seek help and advice, go to www.vincehafeli.com and message me, and I will help you in any way I can.

References

American Foundation for Suicide Prevention. (2023). *Suicide Statistics.* https://afsp.org/suicide-statistics/

Boss, R. (2020, January 28). Death by suicide: Construction workers at risk. *Rough Notes, 163*(2), 40-59.

Brodsky, C. M. (1977). Suicide attributed to work. *Suicide and Life-Threatening Behavior, 7*(4), 216-229.

Cassano, P., & Fava, M. (2002). Depression and public health: An overview. *Journal of Psychosomatic Research, 53*(4), 849-857. (Depression and mental disorders and diabetes, renal disease, and obesity and nutritional disorders)

Carson J. Spencer Foundation. (2015). *A construction industry blueprint: Suicide prevention in the workplace.* Carson J. Spencer Foundation Denver, CO.

Centers for Disease Control and Prevention (CDC). (2020). *Partnering to prevent suicide in the construction industry: Building hope and a road to recovery.* CDC. Retrieved 7 July 2023 from https://blogs.cdc.gov/niosh-science-blog/2020/09/09/suicide-in-construction/

Janssen, P. M., Bakkar, A. B., Jong, Ad de. (2001). A test and refinement of the Demand-Control-Support Model in the construction industry. *International Journal of Stress Management, 8*, 315-331.

Kuo, C.-Y., Liao, S.-C., Lin, K.-H., Wu, C.-L., Lee, M.-B., Guo, N.-W., & Guo, Y. L. (2012). Predictors for suicidal ideation after occupational injury. *Psychiatry Research, 198*(3), 430-435.

Law, Y. W., Yip, P. S. F., Zhang, Y., & Caine, E. D. (2014). The chronic impact of work on suicides and under-utilization of psychiatric and psychosocial services. *Journal of Affective Disorders, 168*, 254-261.

McCarthy, E., DeViva, J. C., Southwick, S. M., & Pietrzak, R. H. (2021). Self-rated sleep quality predicts incident suicide ideation in U.S. military veterans: Results from a 7-year, nationally representative, prospective cohort study. *Journal of Sleep Research.*

McIntosh, W. L., Spies, E., Stone, D. M., Lokey, C. N., Trudeau, A.-R. T., & Bartholow, B. (2016). Suicide rates by occupational group—17 states, 2012. *Morbidity and Mortality Weekly Report, 65*(25), 641-645.

Meltzer, H., Bebbington, P., Brugha, T., Jenkins, R., McManus, S., & Stansfeld, S. (2010). Job insecurity, socio-economic circumstances and depression. *Psychological Medicine, 40*(8), 1401-1407.

Peterson C. S. A., Li, J., Schumacher P. K., Yeoman, K., Stone, D. M. (2020). Suicide rates by industry and occupation - National violent death reporting system, 32 states, 2016. *Morbidity and Mortality Weekly Report, 69*, 57-62. http://dx.doi.org/10.15585/mmwr.mm6903a1

Rancans, E., Salander Renberg, E., & Jacobsson, L. (2001). Major demographic, social and economic factors associated to suicide rates in Latvia 1980-98. *Acta Psychiatrica Scandinavica, 103*(4), 275-281.

Shah, S. S. N. H., Laving, A., Okech-Helu, V. C., & Kumar, M. (2021). Depression and its associated factors: Perceived stress, social support, substance use and related sociodemographic risk factors in medical school residents in Nairobi, Kenya. *BMC Psychiatry, 21.*

References

Simonson, K. (2020). *The economic impact of construction in the United States.* https://www.agc.org/sites/default/files/Files/Construction%20Data/FL.pdf

Turvey, C., Stromquist, A., Kelly, K., Zwerling, C., & Merchant, J. (2002). Financial loss and suicidal ideation in a rural community sample. *Acta Psychiatry Scandinavica, 106*(5), 373-380.

Yaldizli, Ö., Kuhl, H. C., Graf, M., Wiesbeck, G. A., & Wurst, F. M. (2010). Risk factors for suicide attempts in patients with alcohol dependence or abuse and a history of depressive symptoms: A subgroup analysis from the WHO/ISBRA study. *Drug and Alcohol Review, 29*(1), 64-74.

Appendices

Appendix A:

Executive Interviews Summary

Seven industry executives working primarily in the highway construction industry across the U.S., focusing on civil construction, were randomly selected to be qualitatively interviewed. One of the seven represented aggregate mining companies produces and places asphalt and is in the ready-mix business. The research questions for these interviews were:

1. What are the construction industry leadership's understanding and awareness of mental health and suicide in the industry?

2. What are the industry leaders doing to address the topic?

The findings of the interviews are presented in Table 1.

Table 1:

Executive Interviews

	Executive Interviews						
	Balfour Beatty	Chose to remain anonymous	Haskel Lemon	Lakeside Industries ***	Tiller Corp./Martin	Milestone Contractors	Vulcan Materials
Location	S.E.	Mid-West	OK	WA	MN	IN	Nat.
Number of employees	6,000	2,500+	360+	---	250+	2,500+	12,000+
Years in business	130+	105	75	50+	75	---	---
Years in the industry	---	22	---	25+	32	38	20+
Union	---	---	No	No	No	No	---
Vertical contractor	Yes	No	No	No	No	No	No
Horizontal contractor	Yes	Yes	Yes	Yes	Yes	Yes	Yes
Is there an issue with mental health and suicide in construction?	Yes	#	#	Yes	#	#	Yes
Programs to address mental health	Yes	No	No	No	No	No	Begining
When did you begin addressing mental health?		N/A	N/A	N/A	N/A	N/A	2022
EAP	Yes	Yes	Yes	Yes	Yes	Yes	Yes
Focuses on overall health	Yes	No	No	No	No	Some	Some
Mental health is positive	Yes	?	N/A	---	No	No	Yes
Is there a difference between mental health and mental illness	*	**	---	---	---	---	Yes
Employee suicides	Sev.	Yes	No	No	No	No	Yes
Initiated mental wellness after losing employees to suicide	No	N/A	N/A	No	N/A	N/A	Yes
Mental health training	No	No	No	No	No	No	No
Written program	N/A	N/A	N/A	N/A	N/A	N/A	N/A
Leadership support	N/A	N/A	N/A	N/A	N/A	N/A	N/A
Who oversees the program	N/A	N/A	N/A	N/A	N/A	N/A	N/A

* I would say that they are one. You would be absent of mental illness to be mentally healthy.
** Today, I am more concerned about their mental state. It has become more critical in the recent past.
*** Lakeside had a strong program. The employee who initiated the program left, and the program faded.
\# We as an organization became aware of this in 2022 after a speaking presentation by the author.
? Do not think about it.

Appendix A

The qualitative interviews did not provide meaningful answers for addressing Research Questions 1 and 2. Fewer than half of those interviewed knew that mental health and suicide were of concern in the industry. One out of the seven interviewed had a program to address the topics, a second had just begun a program after losing an employee to suicide, and none provided mental health training.

To gather better answers to the questions, I then purposefully targeted the leaders of 15 organizations. Eleven of the 15 agreed to be interviewed. A summary of those interviews is presented in Table 2.

Table 2: Purposely Targeted Executive Interviews

	Absolute Caulking & Waterproofing	Apollo Mechanical (HVAC)	Pacific Northwest General Contractor	DPR	Jordan Foster	Mid-City Electric	Hensel Phelps	Mosites	Shamrock Electric	Murphy	RK Industries
Location	CO	Mult	Mult.	Nat.	TX	OH	Nat.	PA	IL	Mult	CO
# of employees (nonunion/union)	44	2,700	900	4,000	700	550	3,500	50/400	16/66	1,000	1,700
Years in business	27	42	73+	33	40+	60+	86+	54	67	115	70
Years in the industry		33	19	20	20	4	16		20+	30	30
Union	No	Yes	Comb	Comb	No	80%	---	Yes	Yes	Yes	No
Vertical contractor	Yes	Yes	Yes	Yes	Yes	Yes	Yes	Yes	Yes	Yes	Yes
Horizontal contractor	No	No	No	No	Yes	No	No	Yes	No	No	No
Is suicide an issue?	Yes	Yes	Yes	Yes	Yes	Yes	Yes	Yes	Yes	Yes	Yes
Programs to address mental health	Yes	Yes	Yes	Yes	Yes	Yes	Yes	Yes	Yes	Yes	Yes
When did you begin addressing mental health?	'20	'20	'18	---	'08	'22	'19+/-	---	'16	'18	'13
EAP	Yes	Yes	Yes	Yes	Yes	Yes	Yes	Yes	Yes	Yes	Yes
Focuses on overall health	Yes	Yes	Yes	Yes	Yes	Yes	Yes	---	Yes	Yes	Yes
Mental health is positive	Yes	Stress	Yes	No	Yes	Yes	Yes	No	Yes	Yes	Yes
Is mental health different than mental illness?	Yes	---	Yes	No	Yes	Yes	Yes	---	Yes	Yes	Yes
Employee suicides	No	No	Yes	No	Yes	Yes	Yes	Yes	No	Yes	Yes
Initiate mental wellness after employee suicide	N/A	No	No	N/A	Yes	Yes	Yes	---	N/A	Yes	Yes
Mental health training	Yes	Yes	Yes	Yes	Yes	Yes	Yes	No	Yes	Yes	Yes
Written program	Yes	No	---	Yes	No^^	No	Yes	Yes	No	Yes	No
Leadership support	Yes	Yes	Yes^	Yes	Yes	^^^	Yes	Yes	Yes	Yes	Yes
Who oversees?		Safety	Safety	Safety	Safety	Safety	Safety	HR/Exe	CEO	Safety	COO

^ After presenting supporting data to the executive team of the crisis.
^^ In the process of preparing a written plan.
^^^ They have permitted us to pursue the topic. They have not come out boldly and supported it.
Mult. – more than three states

Appendix A

Those purposely targeted did provide answers to the research questions. Each organization acknowledged that there is an issue with mental health and suicide in construction and had plans in place to address mental health and suicide.

Seven of the 11 interviewed had lost at least one employee to suicide. Five of the seven instituted their mental health awareness program after losing an employee.

Ten of the 11 interviewed focus on Total Workers' Health (TWH), including mental and physical health.

All acknowledge that leadership support is necessary and is part of their culture. One did report that leadership allowed the organization to pursue the topic but did not boldly support it.

The organizations began addressing this topic in 2008 and, most recently, in 2022. Most began addressing the topic post-2016 when the CDC, for the first time, reported suicide numbers for the construction industry.

A distinct difference between those selected and those purposely targeted is the industry segment they work in. Those purposely targeted all work in the vertical construction segment, with two of the 11 working in both horizontal and vertical.

Appendix B:
Resources for Employers, Unions, and Multiemployer Plans

- **Man on a Mission**
  www.vincehafeli.com

- **TEDx Talk "Discussing Mental Health and Suicide in Construction**
  https://youtu.be/zrNdAT2vuaI

- **Centers for Disease Control and Prevention Suicide Technical Package**
  www.cdc.gov/violenceprevention/pdf/suicideTechnicalPackage.pdf

- **Construction Financial Management Association Suicide Prevention in Construction**
  www.cfma.org/news/content.cfm?ItenNumber=4573&navItemNumber=4643

- **Man Therapy**
  www.mantherapy.org

- **Mates in Construction (Australia)**
  http://matesinconstruction.org.au

- **Mental Health First Aid**
  www.mentalhealthfirstaid.org

- **National Action Alliance for Suicide Prevention**
  https://theactionalliance.org/communities/workplace

- **Safe Build Alliance Mental Health & Suicide Prevention**
  http://safebuildalliance.com/resources/mental-health-suicide-prevention

- **Working Minds Suicide Prevention in the Construction Workplac**
  www.constructionworkingminds.org/index.html

- **American Foundation for Suicide Prevention**
  www.afsp.org

- **Construction Industry Alliance for Suicide Prevention**
  www.preventconstructionsuicide.com

About the Author

Vince Hafeli, D.B.A. is a practitioner-scholar who holds a Doctorate of Business Administration from the University of South Florida MUMA College of Business, where his research focused on mental health and suicide in the construction industry along with the impact on coworkers, friends, and family members.

He has worked in the construction industry since 1985 and is president of a mid-sized asphalt paving and manufacturing company in Southwest Florida, overseeing operations with 500 employees.

He is an international speaker, author, and mental health and suicide advocate dedicated to raising awareness about the importance of mental health and reducing the stigma associated with mental illness. With a personal passion for mental health and a deep understanding of the challenges faced by those struggling with mental health issues, Vince has become a leading voice in the advocacy community.

He has dedicated his time and resources to promoting mental health awareness and reducing the stigma associated with mental illness. He works with organizations and advocacy groups to help break down the barriers preventing people from seeking mental health help.

As a speaker, Vince is known for his thought-provoking and impactful keynote talks on mental health and suicide prevention.

Made in the USA
Coppell, TX
14 March 2024

30120772R00066